Controlling

Voices

Controlling

Voices

*Intellectual Property, Humanistic
Studies, and the Internet*

With a Foreword by Jay David Bolter

TyAnna K. Herrington

Southern Illinois University Press
Carbondale and Edwardsville

Library of Congress Cataloging-in-Publication Data

Herrington, TyAnna K., 1955–
    Controlling voices : intellectual property, humanistic studies, and the
    Internet / TyAnna K. Herrington ; with a foreword by Jay David Bolter.
        p. cm.
    Includes bibliographical references and index.
        1. Copyright and electronic data processing—United States. 2. Internet
    (Computer network)—Law and legislation—United States. I. Title.

    KF3030.1 .H47 2001
    346.7304'8—dc21   00-056287
    ISBN 0-8093-2372-9 (cloth : alk. paper)
    ISBN 0-8093-2373-7 (paper : alk. paper)

The paper used in this publication meets the minimum requirements of
American National Standard for Information Sciences—Permanence of
Paper for Printed Library Materials, ANSI Z39.48-1992. ♾

For my parents, Pat and Jack Herrington

Contents

Foreword   ix
   Jay David Bolter
Acknowledgments   xiii

Introduction   1

Part One: The Law
   1. Protective Control for Intellectual Products   27
   2. Copyrights and Duties   35
   3. Fair Use, Access, and Cultural Construction   59
   4. Law and Policy: The Balance in Cyberspace   77

Part Two: Ideology and Power
   5. Controlling Construction: The Internet, Law, and
      Humanistic Studies   87
   6. Controlling Ideologies: The Internet, Law, and
      Humanistic Studies   112
   7. The New Millennium and Controlling Voices   129

Notes   157
Works Cited   159
Index   167

Foreword

Clayton Moore was the Lone Ranger. He played the masked man for much of the 1950s on television, providing children with what he regarded as a role model for American justice and heroism. We need not worry for the moment about the rightness of that model; Moore sincerely believed in what he was doing, and for years after the cancellation of the show, he continued to make appearances at shopping malls and elsewhere in this role. In the late 1970s, however, the Wrather Corporation, which still owned the rights to the series and the title character, obtained a court injunction that stopped Moore from appearing in his characteristic mask. Because Wrather was negotiating the movie rights for a remake of the *Lone Ranger*—a movie that flopped at the box office—Moore had to trade in his mask for a pair of sunglasses.

Everyone has his or her favorite example of the extraordinary assertions of intellectual property that have been made in recent decades. There was the effort by the Internet toy marketer Etoys to shut down the avant-garde art website etoy.com, which happened to show sexually explicit art that might upset the young clients of Etoys or their parents. There were attempts in the mid-1990s by the Church of Scientology to limit criticism on the Internet apparently on the basis of the claim that the church's religious documents were trade secrets. (The layperson might well be surprised to learn that a church could have trade secrets; but as we have known since the 1920s that business is the American religion, it is perhaps natural that American religions should also be businesses.) Finally, there are the ongoing claims for ownership of life forms or of the scientific characterizations of life: patented bacteria and mice and patent claims for the human genome itself. The notion of ownership of intellectual activity seems to be growing stronger and to be extending to more and more domains. It sometimes seems that economic entities in our society have the ultimate goal of copyrighting and branding all representational practice and much of the physical world as well. There may soon be no phrase that we can speak, no mark that we can make on paper or a computer screen, without owing a licensing fee.

Ironically, there are good theoretical reasons for believing that in an era of electronic communication our commitment to intellectual property should be diminishing. Many new media theorists, including myself, have argued that the idea of copyright was formed to suit the technology of print. The printing press made it possible both to fix a text more precisely than ever before and to produce many identical copies. Our legal and cultural assumption that an author should own the expression of his or her ideas developed slowly in the centuries following the invention of printing. Although it was not print technology itself that brought forth this assumption—European and North American society promoted the idea of copyright for a variety of historical reasons—nevertheless, print technology would seem to be a necessary precondition. Today, electronic technology should therefore offer the opportunity for a change in our cultural assumption. Electronic texts are unstable, and they are constituted through a cooperative relationship between the original author or authors and subsequent readers. As we do more of our work on computer screens, we should be inclined to understand both verbal and audiovisual texts as collective experiences. We should be increasingly skeptical of claims by individuals and corporations to own texts that are themselves the products of interactions among current and earlier texts, authors, and readers.

What is wrong with this argument? I am still not sure. Perhaps in the long run, excessive claims of ownership will indeed wither away. Nothing in our current situation, however, suggests that entertainment corporations are going to curtail their efforts to copyright the world. Nothing suggests that governments in the industrialized world are going to stop supporting these corporate efforts nor that the courts are going to adopt a new, appropriately electronic view of intellectual property. We face an ongoing struggle over the construction of intellectual property—a struggle for control in which, as academics, we occupy a weak position against these corporate and governmental forces.

We academics are used to dealing with publishers of printed books and journals. Publishers have always tried to make as much as they can of their intellectual property, as we would expect, but they have traditionally had a cordial and reciprocal relationship with the academic community. We write their books, and we direct our students to buy their books. The new digital media are different, for they are, in general, extensions of traditional audiovisual media, which are controlled by large entertainment corporations who are not used to working with the academic community. Their traditional audiences are consumers, not students. Their media are not tied to education, as books are. Sony does not, after all, need teachers to compel children to watch their movies or buy their CDs.

I wonder whether the entertainment corporations are really concerned about the kind of fair use that we as educators actually practice. They are of course concerned about large-scale piracy for consumer markets. But would it really damage Dreamworks economically if teachers were allowed to rent a video of *Jurassic Park* and show it to a class? (Indeed, how many professors even know that Dreamworks would regard a classroom showing as an unlicensed use of their property?) Such corporations favor blanket prohibitions on fair use, perhaps because they simply cannot be bothered to recognize the small (but socially beneficial) uses that educators make of their property. We as educators find ourselves caught in a battle that is really being waged on an international scale among corporations, consumers, and governments.

It is for this very reason that the book you are about to read is so important. Ty Herrington speaks to us as academics and writers about the great and rather silent struggle over the construction of property in an age of electronic media. How can I call it silent? At close range, there is noisy debate in the courts, legislatures, and various world forums. Landmark trials are testing electronic copyright and patent rights. Legislatures are moving to extend copyright. The World Trade Organization and other international bodies are meeting to balance trade interests of the industrialized world against the needs of third-world countries for access to electronic information and entertainment. Yet the struggle is silent in the sense that the general audience of readers and viewers is neither overly concerned about nor perhaps adequately represented in any of these forums. There has been no public outcry in support of fair use. In fact, not only does the public fail to protest legal and legislative actions that would curtail its access to intellectual property, it also tends to ignore the resulting laws. People copy and exchange software and CDs without concern for or even knowledge of the requirements of licensing agreements, to which they are supposedly a party. Perhaps our culture's understanding of intellectual property has indeed changed as new electronic technologies have become available, even though the legal construction has not. The gap between the law and cultural practice is quietly growing wider.

As educators, however, we cannot afford to ignore the efforts of companies and governments to restrict fair use of intellectual property. We have more to lose than the general public, because we are both consumers and creators of such property and because our work requires access to a variety of written and (increasingly) audiovisual sources. Academic work, both teaching and research, constantly demonstrates the interconnectedness of current and historical texts. We must be able to cite, quote, and critique texts in order to forge intertextual documents for our colleagues and our students. We must understand the current legal situation in order to fight intelligently for our interests and those of our students.

For this very reason, Herrington's book should be required reading for academics, especially those in the humanities. The author explains the legal definitions and issues with care and clarity; she demystifies the complexities of constitutional and statutory law concerning copyright and intellectual property. Just as important, she shows how various interest groups seek to manipulate the debate by controlling the legal terms through which the debate is conducted. She argues persuasively that our society needs to weigh the economic interests of the owners of intellectual work against the larger academic and public interests in making this work available. She demonstrates that the problem is too important to be left to the lawyers, who are trained to think in narrow legal terms and who are also too much under the influence of the Romantic notion of authorship. As lawyers, they do not allow themselves to reflect on the irony that the Romantic notion of the creative individual is now being exploited to favor the economic interests of media giants at the expense of individual creators, readers, and viewers.

New digital technologies offer new opportunities for teaching and for scholarly research, yet these opportunities could be curtailed if the balance between ownership and fair use is upset. To redress that balance, we educators must be prepared with the legal facts and aware of the cultural issues.

—Jay David Bolter

Acknowledgments

No work is ever created in isolation, and this book is no exception. I am indebted to Karl Kageff at Southern Illinois University Press for his efforts in managing and enabling this project, to Dennis Patterson and Laura Gurak for their sound review and comments about the book in development, and to my friends, colleagues, and students, who have patiently indulged my countless declarations about the importance of intellectual property law.

I am especially thankful to Jay David Bolter for his continued interest in pursuing answers to difficult questions in intellectual property and for contributing the foreword to this book, to L. Ray Patterson and Stanley Lindberg for their book, *The Nature of Copyright,* which helped me to see the importance of intellectual property policy to our national character, and particularly to Sam Dragga for his extensive criticism and support of this book from its inception. Finally, I thank my parents, Pat and Jack Herrington, for continuing to support me in this and every effort I undertake.

Controlling
Voices

Introduction

R eality exists only in shared perception, and this perception depends
on information developed through the process of creating knowledge. Those who have access to knowledge and control its use and dissemination thus control what we perceive: ultimately, our shared reality. As participants in our nation, we not only must understand how
those in power control information, how they develop authority to control information, and what effect that control can have on our national
culture; we must also actively support interpretations of intellectual
property law that ensure egalitarian access to the information that makes
up our national character.

This book examines issues surrounding how information is controlled
and knowledge is created and explores how that control plays out under our current U.S. intellectual property law. The title, *Controlling
Voices,* provides a map to the book's content; it plays on the word *controlling* by animating intermittently the adjective form, then the verb
form: controlling voices are those that determine how the law is read,
but they also control the voices of those who have no power to interpret the law. In its descriptive form, *controlling law* is that which determines our actions regarding access and information control, but in its
verb form, the action of controlling law is wielded only by those with
power to do so.

The law affects and is affected by issues of control in several ways:
controlling law determines which interpretations of statutory and case
law control the outcome of intellectual property cases and influences the
legislative process; communities' dominant ideologies determine how
they control information transfer and knowledge development; and
individuals or groups in powerful positions, regardless of whether their
power is economic, political, or traditional, impose their own ideologies in the processes of controlling information and knowledge creation.

Individuals' and communities' ideologies affect their approaches to intellectual property. Ideology, an individual's or community's belief in how knowledge is created, is inherently tied to issues regarding intellectual property law because governmental regulation of how knowledge is created and disseminated is at the core of the law. A community with a foundational, authoritarian ideology will support a protectionist interpretation of the law treating intellectual products, but a community whose dominant ideology is constructionist will be more likely to support greater public access to the intellectual products that influence knowledge creation. Since dissimilar ideologies such as these influence interpretations of and response to the law in different ways, we must determine who controls the way we treat knowledge production and how their ideologies affect it. By examining who controls knowledge creation and dissemination, we can also determine whose voices are heard or silenced in the process of developing the knowledge that ultimately molds our national character. In essence, those who control information and knowledge production also control our national culture.

Controlling Voices focuses in particular on why and how intellectual property law is important for educators in humanities and social sciences fields such as rhetoric and technical communication, law and technology, science and technology studies, composition, cultural studies, mass communication, history of technology, human systems, public policy, communications studies, and others. Intellectual property law should be of particular interest to educators because they depend on access to intellectual work as a basis of teaching and also produce a wide spectrum of creative products that are subject to intellectual property law. But understanding intellectual property is also essential to users and producers of intellectual products in other fields and to the public as a whole. Intellectual products not only influence society but embody society. Newspapers, books, office memos, corporate guidelines, annual reports, software interfaces, applications and games, television programs, music, movies, dramatic productions, telephone books, artwork, and the many other forms of knowledge and intellectual expression that describe us as a culture and a nation are subject to intellectual property law. These intellectual products also make up, in large part, culture itself. Our ability to access them for learning and criticism in order to understand them and their influence and to speak to their meaning in our cultural development is fundamental to our ability to participate in society. Those who control the law also control the way society is represented and may effectively silence less powerful groups or individuals who have no access to intellectual products for learning or for criticizing how these products describe us.

Lawyers, judges, and legislators face growing difficulties in interpreting and influencing the development of intellectual property law as it is applied to products treated on the Internet. On the one hand, the Internet provides a healthy new publishing venue that allows anyone with a computer and a modem to introduce his or her own intellectual products to a society of Internet users who span the globe; it also allows them to speak about the works of others. On the other hand, the Internet also provides simple means for copying and disseminating copyright-, trademark-, and sometimes even patent-protected work. The result is that many intellectual property lawyers fear the potential for widespread intellectual property law violation. With their clients' interests at heart, they and legislators who have been trained to protect clients' interests or have no training in intellectual property law at all have followed the tendency to support a protectionist trend in influencing recent developments in intellectual property law. The public's interest in maintaining access to information to support learning and to serve as a basis of free speech has been virtually ignored. But we need a well-balanced discussion on intellectual property issues to ensure that our national culture will be able to develop in a way that reflects the public character of all of society rather than only its corporate representatives. In particular, educators, who have a special interest in advancing learning by accessing information, must participate in discussion of these issues to provide balance from the point of view of policy. This book attempts to explain the intellectual property law and to illustrate that despite argument that the Internet requires greater security against using copyrighted information, the constitutional provision supports public access to copyrighted knowledge. With this in mind, it is also a request that educators actively shape the development of intellectual property law, particularly as it is affected by the Internet.

The intellectual property provision of the U.S. Constitution supports a balance between the needs of authors and the rights of the public to access information. Unfortunately, the protectionist backlash resulting from the introduction and widespread use of the Internet has created an imbalance between the voices heard regarding our current intellectual property law. As I explain in more detail later in this introduction, the courts and legislators hear little argument that opposes protectionist interpretations of the current law and legislation that supports protectionist amendments to the copyright statute. In great part, this occurs because few educators and individuals whose voices would give balance are aware of the importance of intellectual property and those who are have little power to make their voices heard. This book attempts to add weight to arguments in favor of public access to information, but rather than encouraging misuse of work protected under the law, the book acknowledges public access issues in the continuing dialogue on intellectual property. In this way, I hope to encourage others to participate in the dialogue that affects interpretation and development of the intellectual property law that ultimately shapes our national character.

Controlling Voices also attempts to provide information about intellectual property law and the policy issues surrounding it to readers who might not want to struggle through complex and difficult legal materials to explore important policy issues on their own. Educators and other individuals who create on-line materials, hard copy documentation, software, and multimedia products including sound and video, have an interest in where those products fall under a broad range of legal characterizations. As a result, they must have extensive knowledge of intellectual property law to determine how the law will affect them and the intellectual products they create. This is especially true of educators, who support the goal of advancing learning and prepare students to produce creative products as well as produce intellectual products themselves. This book reflects two main goals: (1) to describe and interpret the controlling law of intellectual property and (2) to present issues regarding control of information and knowledge creation that are at the core of the policy concerns behind the law and frame them within the concerns of educators. Controlling knowledge is necessary for gaining and maintaining power, particularly when information is becoming our nation's greatest commodity. For this reason, everyone needs to gain an understanding of intellectual property law, which regulates who controls information and how it is controlled. *Controlling Voices* asks that educators in humanistic fields participate in actively shaping the developing intellectual property law so that power gained by controlling information can be dispersed across a wide representation of the nation's population.

Controlling Law

Judges, lawyers, and legal scholars use the term *controlling law* to describe the applicable law or most applicable interpretation of law to a given case situation. Controlling law in an intellectual product provides legal authority to decide how or whether information is disseminated, who is allowed access to information, and what can be done with that information. Battles over how we should treat intellectual expressions under the law arise because opposing legal opinions differ on interpretation of what the controlling law *is*. As it is with all U.S. law, federal statutes treating intellectual property issues must comply with the Constitution, our primary controlling law. The constitutional law is based on legal policy, which guides our government in managing public affairs as well as pursuing its legislative goals. "This term, as applied to a law, ordinance, or rule of law denotes its general purpose or tendency considered as directed to the welfare or prosperity of the state or community" (*Black's Law Dictionary* 1041). Public policy is

> that principle of law which holds that no subject can lawfully do that which has a tendency to be injurious to the public or against the public good. The principles under which the freedom of contract or private dealings is restricted by law for the good of the community. The term "policy," as applied to a statute, regulation, or rule of law, course of action, or the like, refers to its probable effect, tendency, or object, considered with reference to the social or political well being of the state. (1041)

In the case of the intellectual property provision, the policy behind it supports public access to information (intellectual expressions) in order to further the policy goal of advancing knowledge creation for the overall good of society. Society benefits when individuals have access to knowledge for use and as a basis of critical comment. For instance, it is in the public's interest to be able to access research that makes claims that affect societal views of cultural identity and makeup, such as Charles Murray and Richard Hernstein's infamous book *The Bell Curve*, which claims that African Americans are less intelligent than Caucasians. If the book's research were substantially accurate and well supported, society would benefit from the information it produced; but access to creative products as a basis for critical comment is also essential for supporting a knowledgeable, well-represented society, as this example illustrates. Creators and inventors must also be able to access existing information to expand on that information and to build new knowledge. Just as Thomas Edison's early and basic understanding of electricity led to inventions dependent upon electricity that he would never have imagined and advances in medicine are built on previous understanding of anatomy and chemical structures, knowledge that leads to less tangible products, like that about community organizational structures or interpersonal interaction, leads us to a new understanding of the world that provides a general benefit to society as a whole. The policy behind the constitutional intellectual property provision is in place to ensure that information remains available to the public so that the nation can grow and develop intellectually. Our citizens can then speak to the efficacy of whether our intellectual base is developed ethically, honestly, and accurately.

The policy intentions based in the Constitution are the first tier of controlling law. The federal statutory law provides interpretation of constitutional, political intent and reifies policy by regulating society members' actions. For instance, even though the First Amendment supports a policy that speech against the government will be protected, the

Supreme Court has declared that its policy intent was not to protect speech that would lead to overthrowing the government. In 1950 the Court held that the Smith Act, which makes it "a crime for any person knowingly or willfully to advocate the overthrow or destruction of the Government of the United States by force or violence, to organize or help to organize any group that does so, or to conspire to do so" does not violate the Constitution. The Smith Act interpreted the boundaries of the policy intent in the First Amendment, and the Supreme Court declared that this interpretation was correct.

Although the statutory law is based in policy, because suits are brought in almost all cases to dispense with economic conflicts between individuals, case law is used to treat legal rather than policy issues. Legislators consider the overriding effect of public policy while making law that furthers political goals, but courts primarily decide intellectual property cases in order to dispense with conflicts between individual creators or creators and users. Parties to law suits over intellectual products usually have economic interests at heart. Commonly, creators ask that courts enjoin users from copying and publishing protected products because illegal copying and publishing negatively impacts creators' potential profit from their work. Creators may also ask that users who illegally profit from copying and publishing creators' protected products pay those profits back to the creators who hold copyright or patent rights to them. Courts make decisions in most conflicts between individuals based on the facts and circumstances that help them determine who has best claim to created work; they rarely consider policy in these decisions. Since most individuals bring law suits over intellectual property issues to determine one's legal rights against another's to benefit from an intellectual creation, these cases often demonstrate little relation to the policy issues that affect public access to information, with the effect that judges and lawyers virtually ignore the policy behind the law.

Essentially, a test of policy would require a suit between an individual and the public or an individual whose rights are representative of those of the public; this very seldom occurs. Yet in 1994, the rap group 2 Live Crew successfully defended against a claim by Acuff-Rose Music, Inc., that they illegally copied the Roy Orbison song "Oh, Pretty Woman." The Supreme Court held that even though 2 Live Crew profited commercially from copying "Oh, Pretty Woman," because they parodied the song in order to make critical comment about the banal existence of white society, their copying was not an infringement under the fair use provision of the statute *(Campbell v. Acuff-Rose Music, Inc.).* The Court upheld the policy of protecting free speech in this case, even though the case was brought to treat a legal conflict between individual creators and users.

Legal proceedings are expensive but justifiable when brought to clarify economic issues and establish rights to profit through use or sale of intellectual products. In contrast, as noted above, the policy behind the constitutional intellectual property provision supports public access to information to advance knowledge, not an economically based right. "The public" is hard pressed to find a representative plaintiff in a law suit where there is no economic gain to be earned and where the proceedings themselves are very expensive. As such, individuals who find it worth the expense to pursue control of intellectual products bring suits to make economic claims. The result of this focus on individual legal rights is that many legal practitioners believe that the overriding purpose of our existing intellectual property law is to protect the rights of individuals in their intellectual expressions. Some even claim that individuals maintain property rights in their creations. This construction of the law differs from that of other legal scholars who focus on the policy purpose behind the constitutional provision, noting that the intellectual property law is regulatory in nature. It is at this point where theoretical conflict and debate arise in determining how to interpret controlling law. For example, in the 2 Live Crew case mentioned above, the Supreme Court's decision clarified whether commercial use of copyrighted material could create a legal assumption that the fair use exception to copyright infringement would not apply. The court of appeals interpreted the fair use provision to preclude the fair use exemption for parody if created for commercial purposes. Had the Supreme Court declined to review the case, the court of appeals' decision would have been controlling law. However, when the Supreme Court did review the case and interpreted the fair use provision to include commercial use as merely one of many factors that determines whether the law exempts parody from infringement, it provided a final interpretive decision and thus, final controlling law. The Supreme Court's interpretation, and controlling law unless the Court reconsiders its decision in response to a *writ of certiorari,* is that commercial parody does not infringe copyright.

Intellectual property law's operation, because it is so complex, can lead to confusion. In order to carry forward the goals of the Constitution, to support society's interests in building knowledge, the intellectual property provision provides incentive for individuals to create new intellectual expressions. The provision grants authors control over their work for a limited time so they can sell it, create new work from it, publish it, or otherwise use it in a way that will benefit them. As such, subject to some limitations, the provision gives individuals legal right to exert control over the intellectual expressions they create, thus supporting a balance of rights of the individual creator against rights of the public to access information. But conflicts between and among individuals over control of intellectual products fall outside the primary balance between individual and public rights. Intellectual property cases that pit individual against individual are a part, although subsidiary, of the constitutional treatment of intellectual creation, but the Constitution's overriding policy does not directly treat conflict between individuals' rights in intellectual creations; instead, courts accomplish this through case decision that interprets law set forth in the federal statutes.

Since plaintiffs bring almost all intellectual property cases to treat legal and not policy conflicts, the emphasis in *applied* intellectual property law (most court cases) is legal in nature; thus, policy issues are, of necessity, virtually ignored. The result is that, even in legislative proceedings where policy should be at the center of debate, legislators most often discuss issues regarding control of information and knowledge creation with a focus on legal argument rather than policy considerations. They develop law that determines control of information and knowledge creation, thus, very differently than they would if policy considerations were at the center of debate. Participants in intellectual property cases and legislative proceedings often subvert the "controlling law" in favor of the *de facto* application of legal rather than policy reasoning, and practical application of intellectual property law continues to be based on current construction of the statutory law. The imbalance in argument treating policy and law affects educators and the general public because legislators and lawyers, as a result of circumstance, tend to ignore their interests, which are supported by policy, and focus instead on the legal issues surrounding individual creators' needs. By focusing on such legal issues rather than policy, legislators and lawyers effectively silence the voices of those who would support a public access approach to intellectual property.

Voicing Control

The controlling and powerful voices in social organizations affect community perceptions of authorship and ownership of information, just as interpretations of the law itself affect the development of constructed ideologies. All communities' social negotiation through dissonance to consensus occurs through a dialogic process influenced by the most powerful forces among socially organized groups. Through this process, communities determine how they view the concepts of ownership of information and the creative formation of knowledge. The controlling ideology affects these communities' *de facto* treatment of knowledge as well as their perceptions and interpretations of the existing law. In this book, I examine the core ideologies that drive the legal community, those of communities that support humanistic goals for knowledge development, and the base ideologies that drive the Internet community. Although none of these communities is absolutely delineated along set ideological lines and members of each of these communities can simultaneously be members of others, each societal group's differentiated common practice indicates acceptance of core ideologies within sometimes loose assimilations of individuals. The accepted ideologies within each community affect how individuals and groups treat authorship and ownership of information and the communities' belief in how knowledge is created. Individuals' or groups' belief in a social constructionist ideology can lead them to accept collaborative and even community authorship and ownership of knowledge, while their belief in foundational ideology supports the argument that an individual author should retain exclusive protective rights to intellectual products. Interpretations of law are based on ideology; dissonance arises when interpretation of the law is incompatible with the accepted ideology of a community in which the law is applied. Legal and ideological conflict lead to confusion at best and misapplication of law at worst. Because the controlling voices that generate dominant ideologies affect treatment of intellectual expression and, thus, the process of knowledge creation, I examine these issues at length in Part Two of this book.

Effects of Ideology

Ultimately, the most significant issue in intellectual property is how we as a nation control information. In the process of interpreting and applying current intellectual property law, some voices of interpretation dominate and control others. Part One and the first chapters of Part Two of this book culminate in examination of this *process* of controlling voices and attempt to answer the following questions:

- What is the law and how does it operate?
- Whose voices are heard when we choose an ideology upon which to create and interpret the law?
- On whose ideology do we base interpretation and application of law?
- Who controls the law?
- Whose voices are controlled by wielding of legal power?
- Whose voices should we hear in the process of determining our national identity?

The overall purpose of this book is to underscore the importance of these questions and to attempt to answer them in the process. To do that, I examine the intersection of intellectual property law, humanistic studies, and the Internet; these communal entities represent areas of thought and action that, when combined, generate intellectual and philosophical conflicts that form a basis for national consideration of our intellectual property policy and, thus, law. Individuals who research and teach in humanistic studies declare many differing viewpoints among and within their respective fields. But on the whole, the growing trend in academic humanism is to accept that societal belief is constructed from social interaction and dialogue among its participants. Educators who believe that knowledge creation is enabled through many minds interacting to form new thought will also support the constitutional policy to encourage public access to new knowledge, once created. In opposition, the majority of the legal community views knowledge creation from a Romantic perspective (Jaszi, "Toward a Theory of Copyright"), placing the author in a role as isolated and individual, notwithstanding the arguments of a relatively few legal academics who question the authoritarian positivist nature of legal thinking and organizational structure (Patterson and Lindberg; Jaszi, "Toward a Theory of Copyright"; Samuelson; Karjala; Coombe; and others). The legal community's dominant view that knowledge is created in isolation and that the creator should maintain exclusive control over his or her work is consistent with a positivist, authoritarian stance but flies in the face of the beliefs supported by scholars in humanistic studies. This conflict between ideologies leads to differences in interpreting the law. Thus, discussion about the effects of differing interpretations and application should be the subject of national debate on the developing intellectual property law, and the introduction and use of the Internet provides a flash point for collision between these two representative communities.

When individuals began to use the Internet for worldwide communication, its profound effect on how we treat information transfer, control, and development could not have been foreseen. Internet communication applications allow quick and easy copy, revision, and transfer of information in textual, visual, and aural forms. Although the array of participants who access it do not always agree on whether information should be protected or shared, the majority of the Internet community uses, copies, and transfers the information there freely. The Internet is a forum for actuating ideological thought; World Wide Web (Web) documents containing multiple links to different authors' sites and e-mail posts containing various writers' materials reify the theory that knowledge is constructed from many sources. But commercial entities that use the Internet to advertise products and invest in the materials that they load to the Web want to protect their digitized materials from copy, revision, and transfer. The physical operation of the Internet creates a forum where oppositional views regarding control of information collide. The very nature of the Internet encourages a clash between the constructionist ideology that represents the academic humanist community and the Romantic ideology that represents traditional legal community.

This intersection among humanistic studies, the intellectual property law, and the Internet, coupled with their attendant communities, generates conflicts in thought and action and provides a generous basis from which to explore intellectual property and information control.

Although participants in academic humanist, legal, and Internet communities maintain varied ideological beliefs and goals, their common interests intersect in creating and treating communicative expressions, whether textual, digital, or aural. More important, these communities of participants, collectively, through socially constructed ideologies, participate in creating attitudes toward authorship, ownership, and property, and ultimately, in generating the power to create and control knowledge. The interaction among these areas can be viewed pragmatically and theoretically.

The pragmatic view provides questions and answers to the nuts and bolts of everyday treatment of intellectual property control issues. Although interpretive in nature, the pragmatic stance is rule-based, centered in issues regarding the range of original works noted under the law and determining infringement of copyright. To decipher answers to questions that arise in the area of intellectual property law, a reader needs to know the laws that regulate actions regarding rights to intellectual expression, the predominant interpretations of these laws evident through academic legal argument and legislative history, and how the laws have been applied and interpreted through case law. Part One of this book provides a basic but comprehensive explanation of intellectual property law.

Part One: The Law

A broad variety of individuals use and produce copyrighted materials in their everyday work, often unaware of the ramifications of their actions for possible infringement of the work of others or infringement by others of their own work. Engineers, technical communicators, computer scientists, architects, scientists, and educators, among others who represent our varied national workforce, use and produce intellectual products such as manuals, proposals, progress reports, annual reports, investigative reports, and other technical documents. They also create nontextual informational materials such as photographs and hand-drawn graphics, software, videos, and multimedia products. In addition, many creators procure information through the Internet, including digital communications such as e-mail and data blocks, in addition to graphics, video clips, and sound bytes. Workplace creators may not be aware of the special category of law that inhibits the rights in the work they produce. Both agency laws and the "work for hire" doctrine, which falls under copyright law, dictate writers' rights to their work and treat questions specific to employees. For example, consider a technical communicator who has been working on a digital manual for her company. While at home one evening she has an idea for including a special interactive video clip. She creates the video piece at home, then uploads it into the manual the next day at work. Her supervisor is pleased with the resulting interactive manual, and the company incorporates this technology into its manuals for the next publication. The inventive employee might question whether she or her company owns the copyright to the new interactive manual. As with other questions treated by intellectual property law, the answer to this question calls for complicated analysis that rests on understanding intellectual property law well. Chapter 2 explains the complex law of work for hire in order to provide readers with a basis for assessing possible legal outcomes in circumstances such as this.

Educators, in particular, are facing increasingly complex questions about creating and using materials for teaching. In addition to creating workplace products such as those noted above, educators also develop materials for classes in the forms of instructor packets that include works copied from anthologies and journals, handouts, tests, and instructional transparencies or websites that may be derived from sources created by other instructors or authors in their fields. The legal argument over what is considered infringement in using these "course packets" is immense. Instructors may also want to use materials procured from the Internet. The traditional treatment of Internet sources as "free use" creates particular questions about what constitutes infringement in the digital arena. For example, an instructor may wish to provide his students with the most up-to-date material possible. He finds an article on the World Wide Web that speaks directly to the issues of the course concerns. The students do not have access to the Web, so the instructor wonders whether he can print a hard-copy of the article for each student without infringement. Although only a court can answer legal questions such as this by interpreting and applying the law, the language of the fair use doctrine of the 1976 Copyright Act provides a basis of information from which to speculate; chapter 2 explains fair use.

There is also ongoing debate over the ability of a browser simply to access a World Wide Web site without infringement. Some legal analysts point out that the National Information Infrastructure's White Paper includes language that, if interpreted closely, would prohibit access to intellectual property on the Internet even though the same intellectual property would be accessible if it were in the form of print media. For example, a strict interpretation of the National Information Infrastructure's (NII) White Paper would prohibit the mere act of opening a file and reading it on the Internet because the act of producing text in digitized form requires making a "copy" of the original work. Although the White Paper was produced in 1996, its protectionist stance reverberates in current legislative expansion of copyright protection, in which the No Electronic Theft Act (1998) criminalizes copyright violation and the Sonny Bono Copyright Extension Act (1999) extends copyright protec-tion for an extra twenty years. In light of the increasingly restrictive treatment of copyrighted materials, instructors may be confused over whether they can make noninfringing uses of World Wide Web materi-als for classroom uses at all. This book cannot answer these questions directly because courts apply the law to the distinct contextual circum-stances of each individual case, but it does provide explanation of the statutory law and case holdings that indicate the latest interpretations of the law.

Increasingly, many instructors ask students to copy and develop sources procured from the Internet, such as communications from UseNet News, Internet Relay Chat, and MOOs, and graphics or text files that they can download from the World Wide Web. For example, an instructor might ask students to search the World Wide Web and vari-ous e-mail bulletin boards for information that they can use in their collaborative analytical report projects. The students will most likely find numerous materials that they can cut and paste into their reports. The instructor may not know whether the students' actions are a violation of intellectual property laws. The answer to this question, as well as others treating educational use of materials, lies in the fair use doctrine of the copyright statute. Although fair use does not speak directly to questions regarding the Internet, it still controls questions of infringe-ment within educational settings. Courts must begin to apply fair use to issues that are complicated by use of technology to provide new in-struction, but until then, potential litigants looking for answers to dif-ficult legal questions should gain a clear understanding of existing law as the best means to understand its possible interpretation in cases treat-ing issues regarding the Internet.

In producing their own academic research, instructors also create documents written for both print and electronic journal publication that include numerous quotations and references to other writers' sources. Many also use sources available on the Internet in print and electronic journal articles and for conference presentations. Instructors may ques-tion the extent to which they can make noninfringing uses of these materials. Again, possible answers to these and other similar questions depend on detailed legal analyses of the current controlling intellectual property law, and answers will not be absolute but only best estimations of what courts might decide if faced with these legal questions. But Part One of this book is intended to provide a basis of information from which to understand the operating framework of intellectual property. With this framework, readers will be able to make educated judgments about general questions and will have a basis of understanding upon which to build deeper knowledge when they decide to pursue a particular question through their own more specific research.

Educators, nonacademic workplace creators, and individuals from the public in general create, copy, and respond to copyrighted work as part of their everyday activities. They are directly affected by the existing law regarding intellectual property as well as policy issues, case rulings, and ongoing legal discussions within and among government and public task forces. Working with copyrighted materials in hard copy form has required little study of intellectual property law, since most educators have followed common practice within their respective settings. At the dawn of the new century, however, individuals, small businesses, corporations, government, and educational institutions are crossing paths in the on-line world through technology. Interconnecting disparate communities of copyright holders and users complicates and demands revision of the "business as usual" approach to intellectual property issues. Where creators developed primarily textual print documents in the past, today they produce electronic on-line documents that contain not only text but audio bytes and video clips. Lance Rose, in *Netlaw: Your Rights in the Online World,* explains the current situation regarding the ubiquity of copying and the confusion surrounding treatment of intellectual property:

> There is a growing confusion about property rights to on-line materials. Large entertainment and publishing companies are now setting up on-line operations. Many of them are finding their own intellectual property assets already strewn among thousands of bulletin boards and FTP sites by others. Companies in other lines of business are extending their local networks to the Internet. They are becoming concerned about both company information assets that may leak out into the Net, and who owns the rights to materials their in-house users bring in from the outside and use in company business. Multimedia creators now use the networks as one of their main sources for audio, image, and video clips for inclusion in their products. They have a wide range of perceptions about how far they can take and use [works] of the owner or creator. (83)

Educators need to know how to protect their own and their students' materials. All creators need to know how much of another author's materials they may use or copy without infringement and under what circumstances the use would be permissible.

In addition, all U.S. citizens should understand how their contributions to the dialogue surrounding intellectual property issues can affect a change in the legislation and case holdings over disputes in intellectual property. In a C-Span televised meeting, "The Internet and Intellectual Property Rights" (hosted by Georgetown University Law Center's Cyberspace Law Institute), David Post, Associate Professor at Georgetown University Law Center, stated adamantly the need for involvement in the discussion surrounding intellectual property legislation:

> And all you users who are not current copyright holders better get involved in that discussion because as everyone here has acknowledged, the interests of current copyright holders and the interests of the public in dissemination sometimes will clash and if we are not as *users* of information participating in that, that is going to be a one-sided discussion.

Another reason that we should be aware of issues surrounding intellectual property is indicated in a response to David Post from Dan Duncan, the Information Industry Association's Vice President of Government Affairs. His comment points to the tension between the rights of copyright holders and those of users; thus, a further need to be aware of past policy issues surrounding intellectual property law in order to become capable of discussing the current issues surrounding the "Netlaw" of intellectual property:

> And that has always . . . that has always been the case in copyright law. There has always been this tension there and I think that's one thing we need to keep in mind that the new environment is not necessarily bringing up a new tension. It is perhaps refocusing a new issue that needs to be debated, but there has always been a tension between the copyright holder and the copyright user and I think we have to be realistic about that . . .

Intellectual property issues are structured in such a way that legal history, including constitutional intent, affects the current law as much as or more than does the language of the enacted statutes; thus educators and nonacademic creators can face considerable obstacles in their effort to understand the issues based in law. They need to build an understanding of legal history and legislative intent in order to perceive meaning in issues concerning intellectual property. As I noted above, practitioners often overlook the policy behind the law, disregarding constitutional intent.

But legal scholars also point to the difficulty of determining original intent within the historical setting in which intellectual property issues developed. Intent is also difficult to apply when attempting to find specific answers to current concerns regarding electronic expression:

> Proponents of the original intent philosophy urge that judges faced with the task of interpreting provisions of the Constitution somehow try to reconstruct what the collective intent of the framers was in adopting those provisions, and then confine their decisions within

the boundaries of that reconstructed intent. The question is, then, if the original intent of the Framers cannot specifically have been to include computer programs among the categories of things they call "writings," is the Congress powerless to protect computer programs by "securing" . . . the exclusive right (i.e., the copyright) in such works to their authors? (Clapes 12–13)

But it is only by attempting to determine the policy intent of the Constitution's framers, of legislators and drafters of bills and amendments, and of judges deciding cases that *any* legal decision is made. As a result, understanding legislative and case history, as well as the laws in intellectual property, is necessary to participants who wish to support their own interests. Nonlawyers are rarely knowledgeable about intellectual property even though it has a direct impact on every piece of information they use or create. Intellectual property issues are described within statutory language, case law dicta, and books and law review articles in which the authors, usually writing for the legal community, make free use of legal terms of art. Without special training in law, most readers find these sources extremely time-consuming and difficult to understand. Given these hardships, even educators with special interests in intellectual property issues make more efficient use of their time by working closely within their own specializations.

In addition, the common use of the new computer technology of desktop publishing, multimedia, and in particular, the Internet has created a variety of problems that influence intellectual property law but have a special effect on educators in fields with particular focus on technology, but the great majority of these issues are, as yet, unsettled law.

 • Print media was disseminated through the slow process of writing, typesetting, printing, shipping, and vending, but today electronic publication takes place as quickly as the author can upload the material and click the mouse. This gives the individual much greater ability to control the dissemination of his or her work. In addition, the Internet allows more individuals to publish their work; thus, it creates more opportunity for copyright and copyright infringement. "[T]he trend is indisputable. A shift toward decentralized operations, made possible by the development of information-dissemination equipment, is under way. The information industry has burst on the scene." (Neitzke 127)

The question that arises here is whether intellectual property law needs to adapt, on the basis of public policy, to the differences in the current copyright market.

- Hard copy print materials included graphic representations in photographs, diagrams, and drawings that have been protected through specific legislative enactments and court rulings. Today the electronic publishing media enable the production of electronic documents that contain sound, visuals in the form of GIF files, and video bytes. Some of the questions that arise regarding these materials are whether they are protected by copyright, which traditionally covered text, whether each part of the document must be separately copyright protected as individual documents, and whether the combination would be protected as a whole. In addition, copyright holders and users have an interest in understanding whether a use of one part of the document (e.g., the graphic but not the text, sound byte, or video byte) would constitute copyright infringement.
- The work for hire doctrine, in the past, made it clear that a corporation for which a writer produced a document was considered the author of the work for purposes of copyright. Today, the work for hire relationship is complicated by the increase in the ability of writers to collaborate through the linking capabilities of the Internet. The possibility for confusion increases when writers who work at home but send materials to a company via Internet may be considered contract laborers rather than employees.
- Instructors often post their students' work on the Internet as links to World Wide Web home pages. Questions arise regarding how the instructor may publish a student's work without copyright infringement, who may be responsible for an infringing work within a student's document, and who may be responsible for the infringement of a student's work by another user.
- Intellectual property issues that turn on access and similarity are complicated by the broader access of all users to all works through the Internet.

This is by no means an exhaustive list of the questions that affect educators, but a sampling of the kinds of questions that the current intellectual property law may or may not answer. The answers for these questions are developed within factual contexts and are only comprehensible through a perusal of issues embedded in common law history of copyright, intellectual property laws and their legislative histories, case law, law review articles, and working group reports. The Association of American University Presses publishes guidelines that are meant to speak specifically to electronic issues, but these guidelines are also general, since answers for questions like those above must come from pointed inquiry into the distinct circumstances of each question. The NII's Working Group, in September 1996, completed a White Paper that has provided a basis for introduction of new legislation regarding intellectual property treatment on the Internet.[1] Individuals in support of public access have criticized the White Paper for its imbalanced protection of authors' rights. It is clear then, how necessary it is that educators be able to participate in developing answers to new questions that arise in our various disciplines.

Controlling Voices provides information that readers may use to understand issues involving intellectual property, but it will *not* provide a legal road map for determining what actions they should take to prevent their own violations of the law or violations of their works by others. What is or is not a violation is determined within a rhetorical situation that includes the facts of the case, policy issues that are current within that particular rhetorical situation, and determinations of judges who are influenced by the legal and policy issues within the particular rhetorical situation. It is not possible, then, to provide a list of instructions that could ensure legal protection to each and every reader.

My goal instead, is to situate the concerns of educators in humanistic fields within the intersection of intellectual property law as it is affected by the latest technology of the Internet. In doing so, I hope to provide educators with a clear view of the policy issues within which the laws were derived and an understanding of the related issues in academics that should be addressed in the current development of new intellectual property law. I also hope to encourage instructors to contribute to the dialogic process that is producing the law, which will affect academia in the future. The Internet's introduction into society has created opportunity as well as confusion regarding intellectual property law and its application to electronic expressions. The academy has embraced the Internet as a means of communication with colleagues and, in the classroom, as a basis for pedagogy, both on campus and in cyberspace through distance learning. The need for information about intellectual property is growing as a result.

Despite this need, research that assimilates the issues in intellectual property within humanistic fields is just recently beginning to be published. In my own field of rhetoric and technical communication, for example, an early work, Carolyn Rude's "Managing Publications According to Legal and Ethical Standards" briefly treats intellectual property issues (1994). Martha Woodmansee and Peter Jaszi's "The Law of Texts: Copyright in the Academy," and Andrea Lunsford and Susan West's "Intellectual Property and Composition Studies" are also helpful in framing a discussion of concerns regarding intellectual property.

More recently, Laura Gurak's "Technical Communication, Copyright, and the Shrinking Public Domain" highlights the need for a healthy public domain. In addition, the editors of *Computers and Composition* and *Kairos* have demonstrated the importance of examining issues in intellectual property by devoting entire journal issues to the topic. All of these sources ask readers to consider the ramifications of "owning" knowledge, focusing on the policies that affect the public domain of information upon which we base our teaching and develop new knowledge. This scholarship treating intellectual property issues has been beneficial for considering the policies supporting academic use and development of intellectual products and has included helpful pragmatic suggestions for how to treat intellectual products within the academy. In addition, discussions of intellectual property issues appear on a Conference of College Composition and Communication electronic bulletin board (CCC-IP) dedicated to intellectual property issues, and the Association of American University Publishers, mentioned above, has published statements on electronic publishing. But the bulk of the literature in intellectual property comes from legal scholars, even though the copyright issue, particularly in its application to electronic discourse, crosses barriers of many disciplines. It may be precisely because most of the research is written for lawyers, legal scholars, and judges *by* those in the legal field that research on intellectual property in humanistic fields is beginning to grow. Law professionals, and even most legal scholars, treat intellectual property issues from foundationalist, authoritarian perspectives that are inconsistent with those that drive scholarship in humanistic fields, and authors in humanistic fields are beginning to produce work in intellectual property that treats issues from nonfoundational perspectives. But because most of the reading from the legal field requires some, and sometimes extensive, background in law, despite its importance to the discipline, researchers in nonlegal disciplines often face difficulty in treating this area of the law, which requires clear explanation in lay terms. I attempt in this book to "interpret" the legal language of scholarship in law, statutory work, and case materials to provide a clear and comprehensive overview of the current intellectual property law.

Part One, chapters 1–4, provides a pragmatic view of the law and legal issues that impact the theoretical stances discussed in Part Two of my study. I treat specific aspects of intellectual property law, first by listing and explaining the legal categories in which intellectual products can be defined, then by discussing the applicable legislative history and case law, and finally, by treating issues most applicable to the needs of educators. I reference specific cases infrequently in order to supply simple, clear explanations of the existing law. Deep case treatment requires extensive recitation of facts and explanation of law in case-specific circumstances that are often complex and in which the distinguishing characteristics of applicable law are difficult to decipher. My intent here is to explain the general principles of the current law in the simplest most clear manner possible so that readers will have a basis from which to pursue more exacting study in their own specific interests in intellectual property. I treat case law within more specific areas of intellectual property law in "The Interdependency of Fair Use and the First Amendment," "Who Owns My Work? The State of Work for Hire for Academics in Technical Communication," and "Work for Hire for Nonacademic Creators." In addition, my analysis here concentrates more heavily on the copyright law, since its provisions are most applicable to the work done in humanistic academic fields. I focus even more specifically on the fair use provisions and the work for hire doctrine, since these areas have a special impact on academic work. Part One of this book defines the controlling law and explains it generally so that a reader new to the law can gain a clear understanding of the general principles behind the law. Since handbooks on intellectual property law are plentiful and these sources explicate cases in detail and treat the intricacies of the statutory law, in this book, I intend to provide a starting point for readers who may be interested in accessing these sources as a next step but first require a basic knowledge of the law to enable them to understand.

Part Two: Ideology and Power

Part Two deepens my treatment and interpretation of intellectual property law by examining the *policy* issues that drive legal interpretations of the law. Academicians who support a constructionist ideology and the concept that knowledge is developed through dialogic communication will be interested in examining the intersection among intellectual property law, humanistic fields, and the Internet. Despite the disparity in the nature of these three entities, there are several commonalties among them that make awareness of their intersection of utmost importance to educators.

On a basic level, participants in each of these entities have, as do all active participants in a society, an interest in both the production and use of intellectual products. Creators in each of these areas produce intellectual products in the form of books, journal publications, newsletters, advertising, e-mail, videotapes and World Wide Web pages. As producers of intellectual products, all have an interest in protecting and benefiting from the work they create, but they also have a need to use materials that have already been created, both to gain knowledge and to help them develop new knowledge. Participants in these areas share dual roles as protectors and users: lawyers work within the adversarial process both to protect the work of their creator-clients and also to extend access to work by their user-clients. Academicians in all fields, especially with the rise of distance education, have an interest in protecting their own work and in helping their students learn to create workplace documents that will need protection; however, both they and their students are also users of materials that help them teach and learn as well as develop new knowledge. Members of the Internet community also produce intellectual products in the form of e-mail and World Wide Web pages and, in turn, are users of the same. Issues surrounding use and production of intellectual works touch each member of each of these entities in intimate ways.

A second, greater commonalty among intellectual property, humanistic academic fields, and the Internet lies in the bases of each of these entities in community. The law, although a series of rules that regulate activities within society, is also a conglomeration of people who participate in its creation through a dialogic process in which individuals and represented groups negotiate in favor of their individual concerns and societal goals. Lawyers, judges, legislators, and other connected individuals who become a part of the legal society are assimilated into a social system with its own discourse community in the same ways that participants in other cultural communities become a part of their social frameworks. Like members of the legal community, academicians and users of the Internet also constitute communities. Each of these communities comprise individuals with differing and often competing views; nevertheless, each is created through a process of communicative interchange through which its members negotiate toward consensus. Where legal advocates argue for the best interests of their clients, academicians and Internet users support diverse approaches to meeting the similar goals in teaching, researching, and communicating on-line. For instance, members of the academic community develop differing priorities in teaching their classes; some focus largely on using new technology in the classroom, whereas others focus on print production; some instructors envision the classroom as a forum for treating humanistic issues, whereas others see workplace-oriented skills as more important. Developing program and course goals and justifying the pertinence of research aims to other members of the discipline often require a negotiation among participants, often to reach a compromise or consensus regarding the specific course that pedagogy or research should take.

Internet users also negotiate for consensus; one example pertains to negotiating the purpose of the Internet's existence. The early history of the Internet reveals that its original purpose was to make discussion of defense systems possible among scientists who were separated over long distances. Through exchanges in which non-defense-related personnel became a part of the on-line community, the focus of discussion began to change and the consensus determining the use of the Internet shifted.

Significantly, membership in any one of these communities is not mutually exclusive of membership in another. The Internet community comprises individuals from diverse professional and cultural backgrounds. Many lawyers are participants in the Internet community as are many academicians in humanistic fields. Membership in multiple communities notwithstanding, involvement in a professional community requires a certain level of acquiescence to the unwritten structures of that community in order to be assimilated, and each community is largely influenced by dominant ideological paradigms that drive the work in that field. For example, an unwritten rule of the legal community dictates that judges are always addressed with terms of respect; an advocate must always address the judge as "Your Honor," and include "sir" or "ma'am" after every "yes" or "no." This use of language reflects the dominant paradigm of hierarchy that permeates the legal community. The Internet culture indicates its dominant belief that the communication forum should welcome new participants, illustrated though its inclusion of archived "FAQs," which contain answers to frequently asked questions, that help newcomers quickly become a part of the community.

Academicians also comply with unwritten structures of the community. Academic disciplines are communities within which new participants learn to mold their work to professional standards and negotiate within the process to meet professional needs. The abstract structure of a disciplinary community can be located through inferences drawn from the study of the discourse of professional forums (Bazerman, Myers). New members comply with the unwritten dominant structures of the field by developing a knowledge of the literature common to the field, learning the common language of the field, and participating in professional activities in the field.

My goal is to take note of the characteristics of the dominant paradigms of each of these communities and determine how these structures of thought affect the treatment of intellectual property law issues and how this, in turn, can affect the way we treat the concept of ownership and power in the realm of intellectual property. The differences among the dominant ideological stances of these entities create the distinctions among them and distinguish them as separate communities. The characterization of each of these entities as a community makes it possible not only to find significant commonalties among the three, but also significant differences.

Last, and of greatest importance, each of these three entities intersects in their common interest in influencing which organizations or individuals have power to control knowledge-making, to influence what becomes knowledge, and to disseminate that knowledge. Whoever controls the fate of intellectual property law determines whether the nation will move toward egalitarian democratization of thought or whether information will become closed off from the public, subject to the commercial interests of corporations that use information only for economic gain. In any era, controlling knowledge is equivalent to controlling power in society, but the potential power in creating and controlling knowledge becomes even more momentous in an age where technology is making information our greatest economic and political commodity.

My analysis of the intersection of humanistic studies, the Internet, and intellectual property law reveals a conflict of ideologies. The compatible ideologies of humanistic studies and Internet communities favor interpretation and development of intellectual property law that supports egalitarian access to knowledge and its development. In contrast, as my analysis shows, because the legal community is guided by the Romantic view of property and focuses on the conflict between authors' and users' economic interests, it continues to rely on a common law interpretation of the intellectual property law (even though it has been explicitly overridden by statutory law). Interpretation of the intellectual property law within a Romantic ideology produces imbalanced access to knowledge, and thus cultural development, in favor of wealthy corporate entities and a class of society with political power.

Part One

The Law

1

Protective Control for Intellectual Products

Intellectual property is such an all-encompassing area of the law because the influences of contract law, agency and partnership, constitutional law, and other areas make understanding difficult; studying the law may be daunting. Regardless, instructors, students, and nonacademic workplace creators need to be aware of the kinds of protection available for intellectual products in order to make choices that are most appropriate for the products they create, given the protection these choices provide. This chapter is an attempt to make some of the complicated aspects of intellectual property law clear; the often intermingled treatments of intellectual property issues are separated into categories to provide an overview of the kinds of protections that the law allows.

Intellectual products differ in their character and form and thus fall under differing categories of legal protection. Among the many categories of protection available to creators, the following are most useful to educators:

- trademarks, reputation, and goodwill;
- trade secret;
- patents;
- copyright.

Although legal analysts who specialize in intellectual property law also include categories such as mask works, character trademark and sponsorships, utility models, industrial design and design patents, invention and patents, and information data, discussion of the four general categories above will best serve the purposes of educators. As I hope to make clear in this chapter, even though each category provides specific kinds of protection for specifically characterized intellectual products, at times a certain intellectual product may be protectable under more than one category. Creators will need to be aware of the impact of the choices they make.

Producers of intellectual products must make the most appropriate choice of protection. To do so, intellectual property producers must understand what choices of protection are available and how these choices provide a barrier against illegal use. Both producers and users should understand the different protections provided by trade secret, patent, and copyright.

Trademarks, Reputation, and Goodwill

Trademarks, reputation, and goodwill can be words or symbols used to distinguish goods and services of one company or of one individual business entity from another. They can be maintained in the form of text, graphics, and sound. Even though this category includes three elements, trademark is actually supported by the legal qualities of reputation and goodwill. Educators not only prepare students to develop materials for employers who carry trademarks, but increasingly they are expanding their own development of educational software and teaching materials, which are also distinguished by trademarks. It is thus important that instructors understand how goodwill and reputation support trademark protections and how the intellectual property law treats both trademark use by nonowners and trademark protection by the parties it represents. Trademarks provide rights to the exclusive use of the mark as a representation of the company or individual with prior registration. Trademarks have no inherent value in themselves but derive protection on the basis of their ability to represent the value in the intangible quality of a company's or individual's goodwill. Goodwill comprises reputation, length of effective dealings with the public, good record of service or product support, or other ongoing positive associations with the public. Although goodwill is an intangible entity, it is treated as a tangible asset for purposes of accounting in tax law, contract for sale, and valuation for stock purposes. Trademarks serve to protect the trademark owner against others who might take advantage of the company's goodwill (represented by the trademark) by marketing similar products with confusingly similar names. They also help the consumer choose products on the basis of the reputation represented by the trademark (Neitzke 55). The core issue is that one competitor is not allowed to capitalize on the goodwill of another.

Although trademark rights are dictated primarily by state decisions and statutes regardless of trademark registration in the federal patent office, there are advantages to federal registration. Registration creates notice against those who would import materials with a duplicate trademark, and after five years of registration, the trademark becomes "incontestable," providing procedural advantages in case of legal action. Federal registration also allows trademark owners to use a protected mark in a national arena whether or not they have immediate intentions to use them beyond state borders. Where two parties contend ownership in a trademark, the earlier registration also contributes to an assumption that the first registered party has rights in the mark (55).

When a corporation adopts a trademark, it should make a search to be sure that no other similar marks already exist or that the intended trademark is itself protectable. Some intended trademarks too closely describe a product that is created by more than one company and therefore cannot be used. For instance, the name "word processor" cannot be used as a trademark because it describes the characteristics of the product itself, produced by many companies; the trademark WordPerfect, however, distinguishes one kind of word-processing software from all others. Not only should a trademark be a distinctive identifier for a company or product, the chosen mark should not be substantially similar to a trademark that is already registered. The trademark should be registered early, before developing goodwill, and it should be used nationally as soon as possible to further establish the claim in its use (56). Remedies for violation of trademark registration can range from injunction to monetary damages for harm to a company's goodwill.

Trademark issues can be significant for academicians and other creators, particularly as trademarks relate to using and developing materials for teaching in the computer-based classroom and for using and creating work on the World Wide Web. As evidenced by teaching packets as well as networking software programs for classroom use such as Daedalus and Commonspace, it has become relatively common for writing instructors to produce new teaching materials, including software, that require a trademark. In addition, when classes create and use World Wide Web materials, there is great potential to violate trademark rights, often unknowingly.

Copying and reincorporating graphics into new web pages may be the most common misuse of trademark, and although this kind of misuse is often a violation without the intent to harm a trademark owner, harm can result nevertheless. Trademark producers who use trademarks they do not own can create assumptions that the work they produce is that of the registered owners. The nonregistered user could easily produce a poor quality work or one that fails to convey the intentions of the represented owner, which harms the goodwill of the true registered user.

The fair use provisions, discussed in more detail later in this chapter, do not apply directly to trademark law since they are a part of the 1976 Copyright Act. Nevertheless, trademark reference or parody for asserting free speech commentary still falls within a framework of protection provided by the Constitution. First Amendment arguments make clear that intellectual products are subject to political commentary.

Where nonacademic creators who produce trademarks will be concerned with protection of the goodwill in their products and companies through protection of their trademarks, both they and academicians should be aware of the need to balance protection of trademark against the need for expression. Trademarks have become such cultural icons that the public has an interest in them to the extent that they form a basis of what we are as a culture (Coombe, "Objects of Property" 1856). In light of the influence of our work on students who may be dealing with intellectual property issues for the first time, academicians should be aware of our treatment of trademarks, both in ensuring that we avoid violations and in that our attitudes do not contribute to a chilling of free speech as a result of fear of legal entanglement. For example, technical communication students often produce assignments that integrate graphics and text. Students often scan images to be placed in their print products and copy or link digital images in their World Wide Web pages and need to know that if they use the trademarked material as a basis for critical comment, their use is likely to be protected, but if they copy material to ornament their pages it would not. In any case, students should learn the boundaries between fair use and infringement of another creator's work.

Trade Secret

Like trademark, trade secret falls under state law protections that vary from state to state, but trade secret is a distinctive intellectual property protection in that it is the only form of protection that relies on a lack of action from the secret "holder." As a result, trade secret is the most fragile in nature. Two elements of trade secret include (1) the need for a secret and (2) reasonable efforts to maintain secrecy. "[A] trade secret is 'any formula, pattern, device, or compilation of information which gives [one] an opportunity to obtain an advantage over competitors who do not know or use it'" (Neitzke 6). The following kinds of work are commonly protected under trade secret law:

- customer lists,
- designs,

- instructional methods,
- manufacturing processes and product formulas,
- document-tracking processes. (Brinson and Radcliffe 27)

Trade secret is most often used in software development. The scope of protection provided by trade secret is as follows:

One who discloses or uses another's trade secret, without privilege to do so, is liable to the other if

(a) he[she] discovered the secret by improper means, or

(b) his[her] disclosure or use constitutes a breach of confidence reposed in him[her] by the other in disclosing the secret to him[her], or

(c) he[she] learned the secret from a third person with notice of the facts that it was secret and that the third person discovered it by improper means or that the third person's disclosure of it was otherwise a breach of his[her] duty to the other, or

(d) he[she] learned the secret without notice of the facts that it was a secret and that its disclosure was made to him[her] by mistake. (Neitzke 26–27)

Protecting trade secret and avoiding legal turmoil is almost entirely dependent on trusting employees with access to secrets. The legal questions that arise regarding trade secret are not in registration or filing, for there is none, but in actions against an employee who misuses his or her special access and violates the secret. To take legal action on unprivileged disclosure of trade secret, the information in legal dispute must certainly be determined a trade secret. The six factors for this determination follow:

1. the extent to which the information is known outside the business,
2. the extent to which it is known by employees and others involved in the business,
3. the extent of measures taken by the individual possessing the trade secret to guard the secrecy of the information,
4. the value of the information to him[her] and his[her] competitors,
5. the amount of effort or money expended by him[her] in developing the information,
6. the ease or difficulty with which the information could be properly acquired or duplicated by others. (27)

In addition, a trade secret should display a quality of originality that distinguishes it from everyday knowledge, though it need not be so unique as to be patentable.[1] A trade secret does not have to be known only to the owner to maintain status as a secret, but must be held from the public enough to make it difficult for anyone but a coemployee to learn the information. In addition, when a trade secret is unraveled either through independent development by another company or through reverse engineering, the secret is legitimately revealed and from that point on, is open to the public. Normally, a dispute in trade secret arises, not while the employee still maintains an employee-employer relationship in a company, but later, after he or she is reemployed in a new company. Employers most often create contract terms that make clear the employee's duty to maintain secrecy in development of intellectual products, and most often these contracts contain clauses that ensure that an employee is legally bound not to divulge secret information after employment ends.

Human nature often comes into play, however, and a dissatisfied employee who leaves a company on bad terms may divulge trade secrets as a means of revenge or simply out of lack of concern for the prior employer. When employees have had a substantial impact on developing information that is subject to trade secret and have been ill-compensated for their efforts, it may at times be difficult to predict the reaction of the judge or jury deciding the outcome of a trade secret dispute. Despite language in a contract that clearly lays out the rights and duties of the employer and employee who divulged the secret, both judges and juries make determinations based on their own considerations of fairness developed through an understanding of the contextual situation, and trade secret cases are often complicated as a result.

Both academicians and nonacademic creators should consider the impact of trade secret on their work. Creators are often bound by trade secret clauses in employment contracts; thus, they should be aware that their employment contract regulates their actions regarding workplace-developed knowledge. Often, a more complicated situation arises when a creator is hired as an independent contractor with a limited term of employment. Independent contractors do not often have the sense of loyalty to a company that makes them want to maintain trade secrets; they are not tied to the culture of the workplace community that reiterates a sense of employee obligation on a daily basis. It is important, therefore, that independent contractors maintain awareness of contract duties on their own.

Academicians in the process of developing educational materials should consider creating contracts in which all creators are bound by trade secret clauses. They should also be aware of the complications that arise with independent contracting employees, as discussed above. Trade secret law is malleable, however, and contracts do not always provide absolute answers to questions that arise; nevertheless, the best means of protection for instructors developing educational materials or software is to create firmly and clearly worded contracts indicating the intent to be bound to trade secrets. In addition, academicians may want to make their students aware of the rights and duties of employees in terms of trade secret law to help prepare them to deal with workplace issues.

Patents

Usually, creators make applications for patent protection when they invent a tangible product such as a mechanical device or manufactured entity. Words cannot be patented. Of interest to academicians is that they may have to choose whether to protect software under patent or copyright law. Where copyright law usually treats expression in literary form, patent law treats processes, machines, composition of matter, and other procedurally based entities. Computer software brings these two kinds of expressions closer together so that the distinction is not great. Although, most often, software is protected under copyright, in many instances patents provide superior protection. Patent protection is also distinct from copyright protection in intellectual property in that ideas are protectable in patent, but only expression is protected by copyright. Patented software can be distributed widely without fear of loss. This is always the case because a patent owner can prevent use of the program by anyone, even if the unauthorized user developed an identical program without being aware that a patent in the program exists. In addition, a patent owner "can exploit the product commercially, using techniques that would violate the antitrust laws but for patent" (Neitzke 1). For this reason, creators should consider the option to patent intellectual products that take the form of software.

The Patent Act provides strict standards for granting utility patents and design patents. To receive a utility patent, an invention must be unique or "nonobvious," new, and useful. Even if the invention meets these requirements, it is still not patentable if it has been described in a print publication in the United States or a foreign country within a year before the application date or if the invention was used in or for sale to the public for more than a year before the application date (Brinson and Radcliffe 22). To be patented, designs must be new and original and have ornamental value but most often are better protected through copyright than patent, since patent protection in this area is considered fairly weak.

A patent in an invention is a property right granted to the developer by the government and manifests in the patent owner's right to exclude others from making, using, or selling the invention. Patenting a product is a lengthy and detailed process that requires precise completion of numerous forms and often the costly advice and practice of a patent attorney. Patents can be obtained only on a product that is novel and uncreatable by a person with ordinary skill in the technology related to the invention. A patent must be approved by the U.S. Patent and Trademark Office, which, upon approval, records and assigns the patent. Patent protection allows the patent holder to exclude others from making, using, or selling any product based on the central idea or concept of an invention and is intended to provide inventors with adequate inducement to spend the time and money required to create new inventions that would ultimately be made available to the public. A U.S. patent provides exclusive protection of the work of inventors for seventeen years, provided they make full disclosure of the invention by way of patent registration.

The basis for software patentability is whether the underlying idea of the program itself is patentable as a new and useful process. Unfortunately, it is very difficult to determine what exactly makes some software patentable when other software is not. The Patent Office has a long history of opposition to software patenting based on the lack of ability of the office to deal with the large number of possible applications and with the content of software, which only those with expertise in computer programming can understand. However, judicial opinion proves out the patentability of software, and most pertinent argument surrounding issues of patentability of software focuses on whether the *content* of the software is patentable.

The most looming problem in patent application is the tendency for businesses and universities to develop similar patentable software within a short time of each other. Since patents are granted to the first application filed, it is often risky to develop software in a competitive market without the capital to invest in the lengthy process of obtaining a patent, often up to four years. Software developers may have recourse based on an argument of "existence of prior art" (lack of novelty in the subject of proposed patent), but reexamination is rarely requested and the competitor most often will choose to litigate the dispute instead (Galler 32). Academicians or other creators who might be thinking of obtaining software patents should consider this option only if the software has a high commercial value, will be used for a long period of time, and could be copied easily through reverse engineering.

Creators have many choices for protecting their works; it is to their advantage to choose that which best protects the particular type of expression that they have developed. While trademarks, trade secret, and patents are often used to protect mechanical and software products, textual, aural, and visual expressions are most often protected by copyright. The following chapter provides detailed information regarding copyright law.

2

Copyrights and Duties

Copyright law is by far the most pervasive form of protection for works by creators whose products focus on communication. Copyright applies to the broad range of textual, aural, and visual expressions used in books, articles, and multimedia products, and includes graphic, textual, and musical representations. All of these are a part of the range of materials that students, instructors, and nonacademic creators both produce and use in the everyday course of work.

The 1976 Copyright Act is the current controlling law for treating intellectual products under copyright and provides the basic tenets upon which the law is built, such as the concept of a limited monopoly and the distinction between ideas and expression. Legal arguments and other areas of law affect the interpretation of copyright provisions in application, and these areas include the following: merger and reverse engineering, substantial similarity, contract law, plagiarism, tangibility and fixation, originality, and infringement.

Some of the defenses against claims of copyright infringement, such as reverse engineering and the clean room defense (used when a creator develops a new intellectual product in isolation from the alleged infringed work), are most commonly applied in software cases, but the concepts and arguments that drive them are helpful for understanding general frameworks of argument in the copyright law field as a whole. In addition, with the greater reliance on digitized information, the issues and arguments in software copyright law may become even more applicable to treating literary work, since its character is changing and rapidly coming closer to that of software products than print products. Software-related issues should, therefore, be helpful even to those who may never develop educational or nonacademic software.

The Constitutional Intellectual Property Provision

Excerpts of the most pertinent provisions and the history and development of copyright law help provide a basis for understanding how courts apply it today. Limiting this information under these parameters should help to clarify the issues for a lucid analysis but avoid an exhaustive analysis of the law surrounding intellectual property, which would provide a level of detail that could be confusing.

The intellectual property law is based in a congressional grant to authors of a *limited* monopoly of rights in their works:

> The Congress shall have the power . . . to Promote the Progress of Science and the useful Arts, by securing for limited Times to Authors and Inventors the exclusive Right to their respective Writings and Discoveries. (US Const, art 1, sec 8, cl 8)

The primary policy behind the constitutional grant is to ensure that intellectual works remain in the public domain in order to promote learning. To further this goal, the law also protects authors' rights in their work. The language of the statute, "by securing for *limited* times" [emphasis mine], indicates the establishment of a public domain. Prioritization of these goals is clear, since the second and third goals, the development and maintenance of a public domain and protection of authors' rights, are necessary as means of meeting the first one (Patterson and Lindberg 49).

Authority for establishing and advancing learning is derived from public policy interests supported by the copyright act. According to Nicholas Henry, "while copyright is in one sense a statute, it is also a constitutional principle" (17). The framers of the Constitution acknowledged that knowledge forms the basis of a progressive society and that information and the possibility for learning should be available to all members of society. Freedom of the press is based on this same policy (15). Nicholas Henry states the case succinctly:

> [C]opyright, as a public policy, is almost as integral to our own government as is freedom of the press. Moreover, it is the only public policy extant which is designed specifically to promote the creation of new concepts, ideas, and theories for society, as well as to encourage their dissemination. (17)

Although there have been a number of amendments to the intellectual property statute, it is worth mentioning the 1909 Copyright Revision Act because it contains major revisions in the law. The 1909 act was born from a determination that the current copyright law was inadequate to protect authors' rights in works that failed to fit exactly under the language of the statute. *White-Smith Music Pub. Co. v. Apollo Co.* became the benchmark illustration of the limitations of the original statute. The defendant used the technology of the player piano to create perforated rolls of music for performance of the copyright holders' songs. The technology made it possible to "copy" original works of music, which the court held were not "copies" under the language of the statute (Patterson and Lindberg 75). Congress enacted the 1909 act to prevent other rulings of this kind, but the act also encouraged a proprietary view of authorship, which in turn motivated argumentation based on the premises of common law property. In addition, the 1909 act created compulsory licenses for musical recordings, now in ASCAP and BMI, expanded copyright holders' rights to include the right to make the first copy of the work, and enacted the work for hire doctrine, the parent of corporate copyright (77–78).

Our current copyright statute, the 1976 Copyright Act, enacted in 1978 and amended in 1981 and again in 1998, brought about significant changes to accommodate the technology of television, photocopying, and computers. The first change was to sever the content from the form of a work by protecting only the work's ideas and not its expression of those ideas. In doing so, Congress acknowledged the change in our cultural understanding of intellectual property that resulted from technological progress; intellectual products would now be treated not as physical property, but as an intangible entities and not property at all. By indicating the change in characterization of property, Congress prohibited the use of common law proprietary argument, formerly used to establish authors' rights, and reestablished the support of learning as the statute's primary goal. Despite some practitioners' assertions that copyright creates a property right in intellectual creations, the 1976 act makes clear that the constitutional provision indicates intent to pursue a regulatory function.

Congress also expanded the realm of the public domain by denying copyright protection for, in addition to facts, "any idea, procedure, process, system, method of operation, concept, principle, or discovery" (sec 102 [b]), even in authors' works. Further expansion of the public domain results from sections 103 and 105 in which copyright extends only to authors' new work in compilations and which denies copyright in work created by the U.S. government.

Another major change in the copyright law was the creation of electronic copyright that protects work that is performed in addition to that which is published. In this statute, two major legal fictions underlie this new aspect of copyright in (1) the corporate-copyright fiction, which attributes rights of works of employee-authors to their employers, leading to work for hire, (2) and the "fixation" of a work by which a work is considered a "fixed" writing, even during electronic transmission.

The most important change produced by the introduction of section 107 of the 1976 act was to codify the judicial law in the fair use doctrine, which sends a strong message that the promotion of learning is the primary goal of the statute:

§ 107. *Limitations on exclusive rights: Fair use*

Notwithstanding the provisions of section 106, the fair use of a copyrighted work, including such use by reproduction in copies or phonorecords or by any other means specified by that section, for purposes such as criticism, comment, news reporting, teaching (including multiple copies for classroom use), scholarship, or research, is not an infringement of copyright. In determining whether the use made of a work in any particular case is a fair use the factors to be considered shall include—

(1) the purpose and character of the use, including whether such use is of a commercial nature or is for nonprofit educational purposes;
(2) the nature of the work;
(3) the amount and substantiality of the portion used in relation to the copyrighted work as a whole; and
(4) the effect of the use upon the potential market for or value of the copyrighted work. (17 U.S.C. sec 107 [1978])

Courts and lawyers have criticized the language of the fair use provision for lack of specificity. Although the copyright statute clearly delineates the elements of fair use, a basic area of contention in copyright law is over what can be considered "fair use." Conflicting concepts of the purpose and nature of copyright itself creates confusion in this determination. The actual effect of fair use limitations is left to interpretation based on the situational context of use, purpose, duration of use, and substantiality of the work used. While clear, absolute terminology and specificity of language are helpful to readers who want exact understanding of texts, legislators have a duty to use nonrestrictive language in making law, because the effectiveness of statutory law depends on its fitness for interpretive construction of the language. A law that is too clearly defined can also be too restrictive and fail to apply to the broad range of circumstances that arise in contextual uses of copyrighted materials. Legal conflicts occur within a context of facts that have meaning within the situational framework of the culture in which they arise; what is appropriate activity in one context may be illegal in another. For instance, Internet users accept as common practice that participants on Internet discussion lists copy complete texts of messages into their responses sent to the list. Although strict constructionists of the copyright law might argue that this practice is technically a violation of copyright, an advocate for the legality of this practice could argue that participants, because they know this is common practice, give their implied consent for others to copy their posts. In contrast, in the context of the paper-based publishing world, where copying another's comments is uncommon, the activity could be considered a violation. The facts describing the actions that occur are the same in both situations, but the context in which they occur helps judges determine their legal status. The language of statutory law needs to be open enough to consider contextual situation in determining legality of action in copyright as well. The result is that legislatures make the language of statutory law loose enough to allow for context and absolute answers (until overturned or reheard) regarding potential infringements that arise in the new contexts of Internet use to be determined when cases on those issues are decided by the courts.

The Constitution also guarantees that no federal government will abridge the powers of states to make laws based on community standards. The federal law, then, must be written loosely enough to allow adjustment to community standards. In this way, assumptions about what is acceptable behavior in one state are not mandated in determining what is acceptable behavior in another. When a statute is worded to allow for interpretation, the courts' ability to produce fair results is more likely. Although there is also danger in violating due process by wording a statute too loosely, based on an assessment of unconstitutionality on the grounds of vagueness, those who argue that the statute is unclear do so on the basis of the difficulty of interpretation and make no claims of unconstitutionality. Courts' original considerations of the legal concept of community standards do not apply to activities that arise through participation on the Internet because they have traditionally applied to communities within physical locales. But Internet commerce complicates issues of community standards and begs for a more complete use of the community standards concept because the Internet reaches broadly across physical community boundaries. Arguably, the Internet brings individuals together into a cyberspace community of sorts, in which individuals participate in practices common to Internet commerce. For example, Web browser applications, such as Netscape, include functions that allow users to copy images or text files simply and quickly, encouraging copying to the extent that it becomes a normal practice within everyday Web use. In this case, the common practice of copying files from the Web is indicative of the community standards; many participants on the Internet do not consider this kind of copying and reproduction a copyright violation. This practice, because it is so common, creates fears in producers who use the Web as a forum for advertising their goods or services and worry about how to protect their work. These kinds of conflicts are the hot points within which new interpretations of the law will take place.

Applying intellectual property law requires a balance, on the one hand, between authors' and users' rights in intellectual products and, on the other, between economic interests of individuals and the public's interest in access. Interpretations of the law have generally been dependent on judges' and lawyers' ideological views. Judges who support a positivist belief that creative acts are the productions of isolated authors are more likely to take a protectionist stance toward copyright and award individuals strong economic rights in their creative products. An ideological belief that creative knowledge results from constructed societal collaboration would lead judges to lend greater support for the public's right to access creative materials.

The subjects of copyright protection are, at present, most commonly literary works (in the form of books, plays, or poetry), music, movies, and art but can also be videotapes, choreography, music videos, CDs, computer software, and other "original works of authorship" (17 U.S.C.). This chapter provides information regarding copyright as it applies both to literary works and to software products. Where patent protects only registered work, copyright protects both published and unpublished works. Copyright arises from the constitutional basis for treatment of all intellectual products; thus, it exists not only to protect creators' rights in their creative expressions but primarily to ensure the advancement of knowledge through maintaining public access to creative works.

Section 106 of the 1976 Copyright Act provides copyright holders a limited monopoly in their work, giving them authorization in the following acts:

- to reproduce the copyrighted expression;
- to create derivative works based upon the copyrighted work (such as screenplay based on a novel);
- to distribute copies of the copyrighted work to the public by sale or other transfer, or by rent, lease, or lending;
- to perform the copyrighted work publicly;
- to display the copyrighted work publicly.

An intellectual product is copyrighted upon publication, as soon as the "original work of authorship becomes 'fixed' in a tangible form of expression" (17 U.S.C.). Only *expressions* of ideas in original works, and not the ideas themselves, are protected by copyright. A copyright ensues immediately upon meeting these requirements and the copyright holder is not required to take any action to achieve protection. It is wise to register a copyright as soon as possible, however, because there are four benefits of filing for copyright registration in the U.S. Patent and Trademark Office:

- Possible infringers are put on notice that the work is protected.
- The right to file suit on a copyright infringement claim is granted.
- Statutory damages for infringement are available in a successful infringement claim.
- Recovery of attorneys fees is mandated by statute in a successful infringement claim.

Works that are not copyrightable include those prepared by federal government officers and individuals working in the capacity as employees of the government. Works in which the copyright has ended are those in the "public domain," in which the public has direct rights. State government officers and employees maintain the same rights under copyright as other citizens, although all creators' rights in the expression of their ideas are not absolute, but subject to two limitations, first in duration and then in the fair use exceptions.

Copyright Control

Copyright control is created in conjunction with authorship and the concept of authorship in the context of copyright provides a specific legal status.[1] The term *author* is used regardless of the kind of work created and, in the case of the legal fiction of corporate and university authorship in the "work for hire" doctrine (discussed later in this chapter), regardless of the "author's" actual participation in creating the work. Composers, artists, software programmers, corporate and university entities, and writers are all considered "authors" under the law. Where the constitutional phrasing of the statute speaks specifically to authors and their writings, the courts have interpreted the language broadly to include the kinds of technological advances in creative works that the framers of the Constitution could not have considered.

The rights of initial authors may change, depending on the nature of their authorship; therefore, it is important to correctly identify and characterize the author or authors of a work when registering the copyright. Authors may derive control over the intellectual product in several ways:

- An individual may independently author the work.
- An employer may pay an employee to author the work, in which case the employer is an author under the work-for-hire rule.

- A person or business may specially commission an independent contractor to author the work under a written work for hire contract, in which case the commissioning party becomes the author.
- Two or more individuals or entities may collaborate to become joint authors. (Lindey 8/2)

Rights to an intellectual product are attributed to individual authors, but a single work may have been created by more than one individual. For instance, one individual might produce the tune for a music video, another the lyrics, and a third, the photography. In this case, copyright control is attributed to each individual author in the part of the work he or she produced. Each individual author would have the right to treat the separate parts of the music video as he or she wishes; the composer could set the tune to different lyrics, the photographer could screen the film without or with different music, and the lyrics writer could publish the lyrics as poetry. This situation is uncommon, however, and in most cases the three authors would claim rights in the work through "joint authorship" in a "joint work." The implication behind the term *joint work* is that the intellectual product is sufficiently merged to create an inseparable, interdependent whole. Legal difficulty arises when all authors, before creating the work, fail to agree to produce a work in joint work status. It is not necessary that all the authors work together at the same time or that they even know each other when they develop their contributions; a joint author can be a corporation or other business entity. But the law focuses on intent of the authors at the time the work was created; thus, if it were shown that one author had no intention of creating a joint work, but preferred that his or her portion remain severable, joint work status could be difficult to establish. The contributions each author makes to a joint work need not be equal in proportion, either in quantity or quality, but a joint author must contribute to the creative process of developing the work. Editing or proofreading does not qualify a person for the status of authorship. It is important to be aware that even though contributions from separate authors need not be equal, without a clear agreement otherwise, joint authors have an undivided interest in the entire work. Deceased authors' rights in the intellectual product pass to their heirs.

Further difficulties arise in joint authorship when, despite intent, the work becomes sufficiently merged to make severability of its contributions impossible. For instance, one artist may have begun work on a sculpture and hired an apprentice to help produce the work. The artist then died, but the apprentice continued sculpting the work until its completion. The stated intent of the artist was to create a nonseverable intellectual product, but the question arises as to whether the sculpture is a joint work. As in many joint work cases, the issues are not simple to resolve and different courts arrive at different conclusions in dispensing with conflicts in this area. The lesson for academicians and other creators is to be sure to establish the intentions of coauthors before collaborating on a work.

Joint work authors are legally bound to an ongoing relationship after the work is complete. They are accountable to each other for any profits received from sale or commercial exploitation of the work, and although they can transfer their shares of the work without consulting other authors, because a transfer of rights in one author does not prevent the same transfer from another, it is wise to insist that all joint authors sign the transfer contract. In addition, in community property states, such as Texas, California, Nevada, New Mexico, Arizona, and Louisiana, any property acquired during marriage is owned by both spouses, and joint authors may be required to account to spouses for their activities regarding the joint work. For example, a writer and a graphic designer combine their efforts to produce a CD ROM and agree to split the profits evenly. The popular CD ROM makes a profit for the joint authors, but the accountant handling the sales receipts sends a single check to the writer. The graphic designer was married and lives in Texas, a community property state, but is estranged from his wife, who lives in New York. The writer must split the portions of the profits from the CD ROM, keeping one half and sending one quarter each to the graphic designer in Texas and to his wife in New York.

Work for Hire

Another complication of copyright control develops in the work for hire issue. The work for hire doctrine is a legal fiction that makes the "author" of a work the employer or hiring party that contracted for the work, whereas the actual "author" or "creator" of the work relinquishes copyright control if determined to be an employee of the hiring party. Creators need a clear understanding of the legal ramifications of the work for hire doctrine because its potential effect on them could be extreme. The legal fiction of "authorship" that arises from the doctrine creates a *legal* rather than *actual* attribution of authorship to an employer who controls the work of an employee. Creators should be aware that in some cases they may not retain rights in the work that they "author."

Under the work for hire doctrine, in effect, authors found to be producers of a work while within the exclusive control of their employer and to have produced the work within the scope of employment have no rights in their own work unless they have specifically contracted for them. Academicians, in particular, should be aware of the impact of the work for hire doctrine on copyright law because they both produce work for employers and prepare students who will work for employers in relationships that could be considered work for hire.

The justification behind this doctrine is that it encourages new and creative work—thus, the advancement of knowledge—by providing economic incentive to employers who invest in new creative, but expensive, projects. Establishing work for hire status is relatively easy when employees create projects at their employer's work site, using their employer's equipment and supplies within an ongoing business relationship; but conflict arises when any one factor or any combination of factors are otherwise. If so, disagreement often arises over whether a work was created within or outside the creator's scope of employment. Employees may create their own work away from their place of employment and on their own time. In these cases, the works created fall outside work for hire status and copyright control goes to the actual creator of the work because it was produced outside the scope of his or her employment.

Another category of employment that is often confusing when employees or their companies attempt to determine work for hire status is commissioned work. There are eight kinds of commissioned works:

- translations,
- compilations,
- parts of films or other audiovisuals,
- atlases,
- "consumables" such as standardized tests and answer sheets,
- instructional texts,
- supplementary works,
- contributions to collected works.

The employment relationship between the employer and commissioned employee is most often limited when they develop these kinds of works. The creator contracts to produce a work for the employer on a one-time basis, and once the work is complete, the employment relationship ends. The commissioned creator, rather than the employer, holds the copyright in these cases. If the parties find this relationship undesirable, however, they can contract to consider their creations works for hire. Numerous examples of work for hire contracts are available in handbooks that lawyers specializing in this area of law have developed; however, since the needs of individual contracting parties often differ, creators and employers should also consider seeking advice from counsel.

Creators have many reasons for contracting to consider their works as those for hire and, thus, relinquish copyrights to the employers. Employers may pay creators a higher fee to gain copyright control, and creators may relinquish copyright to a potential employer to create hiring incentive and to develop the opportunity for future work, which can be more immediately valuable than copyright benefits.

Further problems with contracting arise, however. When the hiring party and the creator contract to consider the creator's work a work for hire, it still has to fall into one of the eight categories listed above to be considered such; otherwise, work for hire status will not apply and copyright will remain in the creator. The commissioned creator can, however, contract to assign copyright to the hiring party, even though the work would not be considered a work for hire. Copyrights may be transferred as a whole or in part, which may amount to a term assignment (e.g., of five or ten years) or an assignment limited to a geographic location such as a state or region. Parties can also assign individual copyrights such as the right to create derivations or to modify the work. Assignments are not valid unless in writing and signed by the holder of copyright or his or her agent.

A copyright holder may also create a license in the work, which allows the licensee to use the work in a way that would otherwise be copyright infringement. Every license implies that the licenser will refrain from suing for infringement as long as the licensee's actions are within the scope of the agreed-upon license. An exclusive license is tantamount to a transfer of copyright and is considered so under the 1976 copyright statute. Licensers of assignments made on or after 1 January 1978 (the enactment date of the 1976 Copyright Act) have the right to terminate their grant of licenses within a five-year period that begins thirty-five years after the grant was made. If the grant also allows the licensee to distribute the work, the termination period begins thirty-five years after the distribution begins or forty years after the grant was made, whichever is earlier. The 1997 Copyright Extension Act changes this term by making it possible to terminate the grant at any time during a period of five years "beginning at the end of 75 years from the date copyright was originally secured" (1997 Copyright Extension Act, sec 505, Duration of Copyright Extensions, sec 2).

Employers will want to take steps to guarantee that their investment in a work is protected by ensuring that their relationship with creators is within the work for hire category, and creators will need to be aware of the status of the work they create. The first step in establishing a work for hire relationship between a creator and employer is to determine that the creator is actually an employee. Because the copyright act does not define the term *employee,* the Supreme Court has looked to agency-partnership law to find thirteen factors to consider in determining whether a creator is an employee or independent contractor:

- whether the hiring party had a right to control the manner and means by which the product is accomplished,

- the level of skill required,
- whether the instruments and tools used were provided by the hiring party or the hired party,
- whether the hired party worked at the hiring party's place of business or the hired party's place of business,
- the duration of the relationship between the two parties,
- whether the hiring party had the right to assign additional projects to the hired party,
- the extent of the hired party's discretion over when and how long to work,
- the method of payment,
- whether the hired party had a role in hiring and paying assistants,
- whether the work was part of the regular business of the hiring party,
- whether the hiring party was in business at all,
- whether employee benefits were provided by the hiring party for the hired party,
- how the hiring party treated the hired party for tax purposes. (Brinson and Radcliffe 64)

A creator need not meet all of these tests to be considered an employee for purposes of the work for hire doctrine, but courts may make a determination of employee status when several of these criteria are met.

When work is created for an employer and is classified as work for hire, the employer is considered an "author" for purposes of copyright. This means that the employer maintains (limited) exclusive rights in the works and can use them without consideration of the creator. Employers should nevertheless obtain an "Employee Nondisclosure Agreement" from creators to protect against claims that the works were created outside the creator/employee's scope of employment (65). By the same token, creators who assume that they are working outside the scope of employment and wish to retain their copyrights should insist on an agreement, in writing, to that effect.

As in other situations regarding copyright law, again, the use of the Internet can complicate work for hire issues further. More and more often, internationally based creators and employers are working together on-line, particularly in building web pages for commercial interests. It is important to note that many other countries, although they have doctrines similar to work for hire, will apply different laws in deciding copyright control. Employers and creators should therefore contract specifically for the rights they desire in order to bypass future conflict in determination of copyright. The Berne Treaty and conventions of international law govern intellectual property conflicts that arise in international forums, and although this is an important area of the law for those who work internationally, its explanation and analysis are not within the parameters of this book.[2]

Ideas and Expression

After establishing whether copyright control remains in the hands of the individual creator or is a work for hire and controlled by a corporate author, it is necessary to determine the character of the work within the copyright holder's control. Although the statutory law, on its face, seems to be clear and straightforward, establishing rights in expression, severed from the idea of the work, is not as simple as it might seem, particularly with the introduction of digitized expression. One of the most fundamental issues in copyright and often one of the most difficult to clarify is the distinction between an idea and its expression. As mentioned above, an idea can be given patent protection, whereas an expression, like a fact, cannot. For example, an inventor might develop multimedia editing software that has never before been created. Assuming that a check for "prior art" reveals no other program of this kind, the developer could receive a patent to prohibit others from copying and reproducing the software. In contrast, under copyright, an advertiser who wishes to market the software might create a television commercial in which actors extol the virtues of the new product. The idea behind the commercial is not protectable under copyright, but the expression of the idea—the script, set, and background music, all set within a specific organizational framework—is. An idea is the intangible content of a work, whereas the expression is the form that carries it. In another example, the idea of the star-crossed lovers who unite in death is a common theme, transcending centuries in expressions such as *Tristan und Isolde, Romeo and Juliet, West Side Story,* and countless others. The idea is not protected, but each separate expression, distinct in its form, is. Although earlier case law pointed out the distinction between protecting the idea and expression in copyright, the 1976 Copyright Act makes this distinction explicit:

> In no case does copyright protection for an original work of authorship extend to any idea, procedure, process, system, method of operation, concept, principle, or discovery, regardless of the form in which it is described, explained, illustrated, or embodied in such a work. (17 U.S.C. sec 102 [b])

Difficulties arise in separating ideas and expression, particularly in original works such as music and software. Judges find it nearly impossible to separate a musical "idea" from musical "expression." One means of making a distinction between the idea of a work and the expression of that idea is in the number of ways an idea can be expressed. "If there are many ways, many choices, then we are dealing with expression" (Galler 24). Courts interpret the law and make case-by-case determinations of these issues on a regular basis, and although legal decision is often based on precedent, the ephemeral nature of this issue makes it difficult to rely on case law.

Merger and Reverse Engineering

In situations where idea and expression are so intimately entwined to make it almost impossible to distinguish one from the other, lawyers rely on the merger argument. Information may be expressed in the form of electronic data in such a way that the data and the expression are one and the same. A litigant might argue for protection of the work on the basis of the concept that to copy the idea contained digitally, the user would also have to copy the expression, thereby infringing the copy; thus, the idea and expression are substantially merged to the effect that copying the idea would constitute infringement.

Although digitizing text creates a potential for merging ideas and expression in a variety of works, ranging from text to video bytes, this situation arises most often in software copyright cases. A typical instance is one in which a creator has produced a video game package that includes the game hardware, the game cartridge, and the software. The game works only when activated by a special digital code sequence transmitted by the cartridge. Another manufacturer wishes to compete by producing its own cartridges. The competitor's cartridges would have to transmit the correct sequence of data to be able to activate the game (Galler 24). If the original manufacturer were successful in making the merger argument and preventing the competitor from copying the sequence code, the competitor would have recourse in an act of reverse engineering. In another example, Apple Computer sued Microsoft, claiming that Microsoft infringed its copyright when it copied Apple's graphical user interface (GUI) for use in its new Windows applications. In this case, the Court of Appeals pointed to the difficulty of separating the idea from expression in a GUI and noted that when ideas and expression are sufficiently merged, the expression cannot be protected. Rather than using the merger reasoning, however, the court relied on Apple's license to Microsoft to use derivative works from their GUI to decide that Microsoft did not violate Apple's copyright *(Apple Corp. v. Microsoft, Inc.)*. Reverse engineering is often an appropriate action for merger situations but is commonly used in other situations as well.

Reverse engineering is most common to users of copyrighted software, since the character of software is such that their patterns of operation can be deciphered through close examination. While loading, displaying, or running copyrighted software, users are entitled, without permission of the copyright holder, to examine and test the way a program works in order to understand the principles (ideas behind the program) that make it work. For example, although the court did not speak to this issue in *Apple Corp. v. Microsoft, Inc.*, the iconic point and click operating system that makes users' interface with the computer simple and intuitive is created with programming language. In the process of reverse engineering, software developers could legally examine the code of that programming language to determine how the interface was created. They could not make a copy of the language without infringing the copyright, but if they used the copyrighted program as an example and independently developed their own code to perform the same function, their actions would be legal.

This principle of reverse engineering has been active since the beginning of technological history but has not been codified except in the Council of European Community's directives of 14 May 1991 (art 5 [3]), which does not carry the force of law. The purpose of the intellectual property statute supports reverse engineering, which, as stated earlier, furthers the advancement of learning by ensuring that the ideas of a work are free for use, copy, and dissemination. The concept of reverse engineering has been challenged recently in software cases because the nature of software is such that its examination requires disassembling the program itself beyond the kind of disassembly needed to examine the function of a mechanical device like a motor or bicycle. Disassembling a motor allows the examiner to see the parts and how they fit together, but tearing down a software program allows the examiner to see the process through which it was created; this procedure produces results far beyond the original function of reverse engineering (Galler 105).

Often the courts determine the validity of the defense of reverse engineering by deciding whether a program was actually engineered or copied. To do so, they examine the defendant's records to determine the existence of a long paper trail, which is commonly generated in the process of reverse engineering. The paper trail is only one element that helps to establish a level of effort, in both software-based copyright cases as well as other forms of expression. The copyright law allows for the possibility that more than one creator can develop similar expressions simultaneously, considering common exposure to the same influences during substantially the same periods of time. In addition to a search for the paper trail, to distinguish pure copy from similar original production, courts also apply the "clean room test" as a defense to infringement claims. Essentially, the clean room test demonstrates that the product was independently developed; since the competitor has developed its own product isolated in a "clean room," there could be no valid charge of copying, which is dependent upon access to another's expression. Although there are no formal elements used for this defense, some guidelines provide a basis for determining the existence of a clean room:

- Occupants of the room have no access to the challenger's work or to any design or materials that would indicate how the work was created. Former employees are excluded from the clean room to avoid negative presumptions.
- The clean room is isolated from any communication between occupants and others who might have contact with the copyrighted work, design, or procedures for development. Even social contact is avoided during clean room activity. Physical location of the clean room away from social contacts also aids in maintenance of an untainted environment.
- The clean room maintains a credible monitor for all information, materials, and equipment that come in and out of the room. Often an independent third party is used for this purpose.
- Accurate and detailed records are kept regarding all information and materials that come in and out of the clean room and citations are noted when new items are produced in order to maintain recordings of their public nature.
- The monitor checks all communication that passes between occupants of the clean room and anyone else who has contact. All telephone conversations are recorded and all correspondence, whether on paper, audio, or video tape is dutifully monitored.
- All participants maintain complete records of day to day activities and progress made.
- The work created in the clean room should be seen and evaluated only at the end of all clean room activity. (Galler 127–28)

These measures may seem extreme but are required in anticipation of use of the clean room defense.

Substantial Similarity

The clean room defense helps to rebut a claim of infringement based on the test for substantial similarity. If copyright holders can show that an alleged infringer had access to the work in question, they can make out a circumstantial case for infringement if they can also prove that the allegedly infringing work is substantially similar to the original. To prove similarity, copyright holders must show that the two works are enough alike that copying was probable. The argumentative issues that arise make this seemingly simple test much more complicated to apply. Two intellectual products, most often software programs, may look similar but include a number of substantial differences that can invalidate the circumstantial presumption. The extent and nature of the similarities in two intellectual products help to determine whether there is a basis for a presumption of infringement. For example, two computer programs may be written in the same language for the same computer and much of the code may be identical, but if both programs' purpose is to create the same function and the code for creating that function is standard, identical coding would be necessary and expected.

In *Plagiarism and Originality,* Alexander Lindey identified fourteen reasons that works might be similar yet not violations of copyright:

- the use, in both, of the same or similar theme,
- the fact that commonplace themes carry commonplace accessories,
- the use, in both works, of stereotypes or stock characters,
- the fact that both employ the same well-weathered plot,
- the limited number of plots generally,
- the presence, in both, of hackneyed ingredients, episodes, devices, symbols, and language,
- the fact that both authors have drawn on the world's cultural heritage, or have cast their works in the same tradition,
- the imperatives of orthodoxy and convention [whether they follow common forms],
- the impact of influence and imitation (both may be influenced by or imitate the same sources),
- the process of evolution (that the likeness is possible because both authors were influenced through the same processes),
- the dictates of vogue or fashion (both authors followed the same trends),
- the fact that both authors have stolen from the same predecessor,
- the fact that both have made legitimate use of the same new item, historical event, or other source material, and
- the intervention of coincidence. (12/5)

Substantial similarity is provable in those instances in which both programs are alike in areas where the programmer has many options. For instance, when a game program contains the same characters, functions, mapping, goals, and graphic representations as a copyrighted program and the programmer had access to the first program, the presumption of infringement based on a test of substantial similarity is strong.

In cases of substantial similarity, both in regard to computer software as well as literary works, the focus must be on a comparing expression in the two intellectual products and not on the ideas, because, as noted earlier, the copyright statute protects only the expression and not the ideas in a work. Focusing on this distinction often causes problems for the trier of fact. Even though many courts consider juries the best judge of substantial similarity, since they most closely represent the possible users of the work in question, jury members' difficulty in clearly separating ideas and expression can be problematic. To avoid questions regarding substantial similarity and the validity of copyright control, software programmers will often include extraneous characters in the software in order to easily catch an infringer who simply copied the program. In this case, similarities in the programs could not simply be fortuitous, which is a clear determinant of the existence of an infringing copy.

Contract Law

Although trademark, trade secret, patent, and copyright offer legal protections for intellectual products, not all these legal treatments are adequate to protect all forms of intellectual property. For instance, a creator might want to protect an idea rather than an expression of the idea; ideas are not protected by copyright, and patent protects mechanical devices rather than ideas. In such cases, the creator may use contract law before making the idea known to ensure that the work remains safe from poaching. Authors may rely on trade secret, as discussed above, or use of contracts to be paid for any ideas used. This situation is not uncommon in entertainment law, where scriptwriters contract with producers to use the ideas for screenplays even when the work has not yet been written. Advertising agents, as well, often submit an idea before completing an agreement for work to be done.

A contract is an agreement between two or more parties, either oral or written, that is legally enforceable. The most basic parameters of a contract include a bargained-for promise or promises and mutual "consideration": in other words, the foundation of an "offer," "acceptance," and "consideration." The offer is the proposal to create a contract and the acceptance is the offeree's assent to contract under the offeror's terms. Acceptance can be in the form of an action or written sign; it does not need to be conveyed in words. If the offeree does not accept the contract, the offeror can revoke it. The offeree cannot assume that the offer remains open and go back at a later time to accept the contract. If he or she needs more time to consider the offer, he or she should ask the offeror for a written agreement to hold the offer open for a set time.

Performing the terms of the contract is not tantamount to acceptance. The contract should first be accepted before any performance is made.

Offerors and acceptors can create consideration in a promise to complete an action, not to perform a certain action, or to provide a benefit in the form of goods or money. Consideration can also take the form of immediate economic benefit through goods or money. Essentially, an offeror and offeree create consideration in an exchange or promise of exchange of whatever the bargaining parties want from each other.

When a party to the contract fails to provide the promised consideration in the form of goods, service, action, et cetera, that party "breaches" the contract and can be held liable to the other contracting party in court. Usually, the remedy for breach of contract is payment of money damages that will put the nonbreaching party into the financial position he or she would have been in had the contract not been breached. Under circumstances in which the only feasible remedy, to be fair, is to perform an action (in equity), such as a situation in which a singer has contracted to perform and the tickets have already been sold, the court may order the breaching party to perform the bargained-for contractual obligations.

It is always preferable to create written rather than oral contracts. Creating a written contract often causes both parties to go through a sometimes difficult process of clarifying their expectations from their intended contract. Unclear expectations or those that the contract does not consider become visible in a written document and can help the contracting parties to either clarify their expectations or not to contract with each other at all. Their agreement will also tend to be more complete and need less resolution in the future.

In addition, once the parties make a written contract, they no longer need to rely on their memories to determine their contractual intent. A contract can be helpful on a day-to-day basis as a reference or for specific needs in the event that a conflict over expectations arises either before or after a lawsuit is filed. Some kinds of contracts require a written document for enforcement; as I discussed in the work for hire section, in the case of copyright assignment under the copyright act, a written contract is required. Some state laws also require written contracts if the sale of goods is for $500 or more (Brinson and Radcliffe 41).

Not all individuals can enter into contracts. Both minors and individuals that a court has declared incompetent or proved to be incompetent within contract litigation lack the legal capacity to enter into contracts. All other individuals or corporate entities are assumed to have the capacity to contract. Corporations have the capacity to contract through agents, officers, and employees, though the agency partnership law becomes complicated when courts make legal determinations of the scope of the agents' power. (When these specific issues become pertinent, it is advisable to hire an attorney; at this point, readers would need more detailed information, in addition to specific legal counsel, than this study is intended to provide.)

Plagiarism

Creators may also use nonlegal avenues for protecting their work so that they can discuss ideas freely while developing copyrightable work for the future. Most universities list written rules regarding plagiarism, including the sanctions that will be imposed if it is discovered, but determining what is considered plagiarism can be difficult. When several individuals discuss the same ideas, interjecting references to both written and unwritten sources, delineating "ownership" of ideas can also be difficult. Particularly in e-mail discussions in which pieces of messages are cut and pasted into new posts and in which the ideas themselves rather than the producers of ideas are emphasized, charging individuals with plagiarism is not only problematic but often considered unnecessary. Jim Swan's fascinating "Touching Words: Helen Keller, Plagiarism, Authorship," points to the complexity involved in defining plagiarism by describing the difficulties that Helen Keller experienced after publication of her prize-winning essay, "Frost King." Because Keller had limited sensory perception, she learned to express her emotions by memorizing passages from stories told by her instructor. These passages from authored stories became Keller's metaphors for expression. When she later "wrote" her own stories by dictating these metaphorical passages, which she interspersed with other means of expression, the examining board that had previously awarded her for having written her own piece, became convinced that she had instead plagiarized others' work. Swan's description questions what constitutes plagiarism, pointing out that all work could be considered plagiarized, since all expression is based on that learned from other sources. Rebecca Moore Howard's "Plagiarisms, Authorships, and the Academic Death Penalty" points out that actions that might be considered plagiarism, such as "patch writing" and modeling, are actually part of the learning process and are indicative of the nonproprietorial manner in which even sophisticated authors treat text. In addition, many cultures outside the United States rely on close collaboration, what we might call plagiarism, as normal efforts in knowledge building. Reliance on regulations regarding plagiarism is not an absolute means for protecting "originally authored" works. Most important is to note that laws regarding copyright and regulations treating plagiarism are two different kinds of protection: one provides strong protection of *expression* of ideas, and the other provides weak protection for the ideas themselves.

Tangibility and Fixation

In addition to the difficulty in separating protection of the idea from the expression of the idea, in order for a work to be protected under copyright it must be *fixed* in a *tangible* form of expression. In the past, when all copyrighted materials were manifest in the forms of books, sheets of music, and booklets produced on printed pages, all intellectual property was fixed and tangible. (The oral tradition of conveying stories and music, in the early history of copyright, did not meet the test of intellectual property, for at that time, property was considered only that which was tangible.) Since then, introduction of digitized text and computer software for treatment under the intellectual property law has created problems in establishing clear definitions of fixation and tangibility.

The 1976 Copyright Act's section 101 states that "a work is 'fixed' in a tangible medium of expression when its embodiment in a copy or phonorecord, by or under the authority of the author, is sufficiently permanent or stable to permit it to be perceived, reproduced, or otherwise communicated for a period of more than a transitory duration" (17 U.S.C. sec 101). The requirement that a work must be perceived to be fixed and tangible means that a person should be able to see or hear the work, for example, in choreography or music, as notations on a piece of paper or on audiotape, in order for a performer to be able to reproduce the work. A performance without the production of sheet music or without creation of audiotape would not be fixed and, thus, not copyrightable, although under BMI and ASCAP, live performances are protected. (This is another interesting area of the law, but detailed analysis of performance law is not within the scope of this book). For example, an artist who has considered the layout and color scheme for a mural would have no protection in the work until he or she sketched the drawing and made color notations. At this point copyright would protect the sketch and the notations but still not the work itself because it would still be unfixed and intangible. At the point when the mural itself is created, it becomes fixed in a tangible (perceivable) form, thus, is copyrighted. Fixation marks the beginning of copyright in a work and protects only those works that are fixed in a tangible form. In some states, common law copyright is still available to protect works that are not yet fixed or tangible, but these protections vary from state to state.

Originality

To merit copyright protection under the statute, a work must be original, which means that the intellectual product must be the result of an individual's mind. The validity of the concept that anything can be developed by a sole creator is already susceptible to criticism and becoming more so with the influence of digitized communication, but for purposes of the copyright statute, the requirement still stands. Originality alone is not enough to merit copyright protection. Facts may be original in that one individual may be the first to discover them, but facts (such as mathematical equations, historical theories, and scientific discoveries) are part of the public domain (Strong 3). Ironically, derivative works can be considered original and copyrightable. For instance, a multimedia project that makes use of the original ideas of others is protectable under copyright even though the multimedia creator did not concoct the graphics and music from an original source. "Derivative works are those in which someone else's creation is 'recast, transformed, or adapted'" (4), as a work of art can be scanned into digital form, manipulated digitally, and linked into a document on the World Wide Web. An individual might also recreate a preexisting work without ever having had access to it, as is often the case with computer programs (which is why patent is often a better choice of intellectual property protection for software).

A creator can also obtain copyright protection in a derivative work based on a work in the public domain. A derivative work is developed from a basis of another work. Because a work in the public domain is available for use without copyright infringement, a creator may use it to form a new work and thus a new copyright. For example, the Declaration of Independence is available in public domain, but an individual's republication of the document, which includes decorative embellishment and annotation, can be copyrightable in its own right, thus protected from infringement. The distinction is that authors of derivative works must invest their own measure of skill in creating the new work in order to contribute to the creative development of new knowledge. A derivative work may be made from a copyrighted work but would be considered infringing unless the copyright holder authorized the derivative. Even then, protection of the derivation extends only to the second creator's original contribution (5). For example, family members of a public figure might collect personal letters and lend them to a museum for public display. An author who wished to copy the contents of the letters for publication would be prohibited. Creators can easily develop derivative work from originals that are in digitized form, since bits and bytes are easily manipulated. The volume of copyright cases dealing with disputes over derivative works will likely increase as creators and users develop more digitized works.

Despite what seems a logical assumption, original works need not be of any real creative value but only need be original; bad art is still protectable, even if seemingly without merit. One guideline for determining originality in derivative works is to question the motive of the creᵃator. If the creator intended to tell a new story or make a new artistic statement in a way that resembles another's work, infringement is doubtful, even though recognizability of the primary work can contribute to proof of infringement.

Other categories of derivative works that can be newly copyrightable under the statute are annotations, editorial revisions, and elaborations. In this case, the modifications to the work have to be so complete as to "represent an original work of authorship" (17 U.S.C. sec 102). Again, the law protects the original contribution and creative modification by the new author. For a work to gain protection, the extent of original contribution must be "substantial," but the law does not state specifically what constitutes substantiality, and recently the rules have been tightened (Strong 7).

An additional category of derivative work in which none of the content is original but still is protected by copyright is that of compilations. Creators of telephone directories, catalogs, dictionaries, and other similar compilations are rewarded with copyright status for the act of collecting and compiling resource information. Infringers' arguments that the content of these compilations are facts (which are noncopyrighted as part of the public domain) often fail on the basis that the format, layout, and design of compilation are original creative production, thus, noninfringing. In addition, advocates for compilers point out that "what is really being protected in all such cases is the economic value of the work put into them. . . . You will be held liable only if you have taken a free ride on the first writer's labor; if, as a result of your own investigations you arrive at the same results, you will be able to get your own copyright" (9).

Infringement

After meeting all the requirements for holding copyright in intellectual expression, the author gains rights against infringement of the work. Infringement is a violation of the rights of a copyright holder by copying, performing, publishing, displaying, or creating a derivative work from an expression protected under copyright. Infringement can take the form of a photocopy, scanned digitization, or other mechanically produced copy, but it can also occur in videotape, audiotape, performance, or display of a copyrighted work. Proving infringement is sometimes a difficult process, requiring that the complaining party first establish a right to control the copyright of the work, then that he or she prove that the work has been infringed.

The most obvious infringement cases are those in which the infringing party copied a work almost verbatim. In this case, use of the access and substantial similarity tests can usually prove infringement quickly and without a great deal of effort, particularly if the copy contains specific markers of infringement, such as the inclusion of the same errors or characteristic markings. Of course, as discussed above, complainants may run into snags when applying this reasoning.

Infringement is more difficult to prove when the accused infringer has changed the work to such an extent that it is difficult to maintain the substantial similarity argument and when the idea and the expression are so completely merged that use of the idea, which is available in public domain, is equivalent to use of the expression. A more common defense against a claim of infringement, however, is the *scenes a faire* doctrine, which argues that common means of expression of ideas cannot be infringement of another's work. A typical example is the formal report format (e.g., title page, table of contents, list of illustrations, etc.) used in technical documents. In this case, the means of expression has become so common to the business world's cultural framework of understanding that its use conjures up connotative expression itself, much like a definition of "technical report."

The basis of conflict in using the *scenes a faire* defense is how to establish what is common or standard, thus noninfringing expression, particularly when many "standard" cultural expressions are born, transformed, and die out quickly. Microsoft Corporation made an interesting *scenes a faire* argument in the previously cited *Apple Corp. v. Microsoft, Inc.* case in which argument ensued over whether the desktop images with files and folders were standard expression or "owned" by Macintosh:

> Microsoft prepared a videotape of user interfaces used in a number of products competing with the Macintosh and with the Microsoft Windows products at issue in the litigation. Relative to the perceived commonalty of these user interfaces, Microsoft argued that the Apple user interface copyright should be deemed invalid because of a *scenes a faire* defense, even though most of the products using the so-called standard features came out after the Macintosh had established its popularity. Very likely those features were adopted because of the Macintosh popularity, thus making it the standard. (75)

Microsoft was successful in its arguments, and Windows technology has become the standard for most software producers. Following this argument, contribution to cultural expression does not itself guarantee a benefit to the developer of that expression. Although the issues are very different, the fair use exceptions to copyright infringement are also culturally based. The following chapter provides a detailed description of fair use.

3

Fair Use, Access, and
Cultural Construction

Fair use provides legal exceptions to the protections established in the intellectual property statute but simultaneously supports an important protection of the right of public access to information. In doing so, the fair use exceptions further the goal of cultural advancement by ensuring society's development of knowledge. The fair use exceptions thus provide direct support for the policy intentions of the constitutional intellectual property provision. Fair use is a means to assure that the information that is at the basis of our culture remain accessible for critical comment, parody, news reporting, and educational purposes.

Educators gain the greatest support for classroom use of protected work from these exceptions. The fair use exceptions, applied in conjunction with the First Amendment, ensure our freedom to use otherwise protected work as a basis of critical comment and as a starting point for developing critical thought; both are of great value to us in our roles as academicians. This chapter explains that fair use extends our scope of legal use to otherwise protected works, while balancing right of access against individual creators' rights.

This chapter focuses on these elements of the fair use exceptions: purpose and character of use, including quotation, critical comment, educational purposes, parody, and news reporting; the nature of the work, including collections and anthologies, video and audio productions, compilations, workbooks, standardized test sheets and exercises, out of print and unpublished works; the amount and substantiality of the portion of the work used; and the potential market value of the work and the effect of use.

Both the limitation on duration of authors' rights in their works and the fair use exceptions to copyright infringement were developed from a culturally based purpose of ensuring America's advancement of knowledge. Even though expression is protected, as discussed above, society is free to use facts, ideas, processes, or methods of operation within a copyrighted work (Galler 112). But the fair use exceptions allow use of the expression of a work as well, in order to support the public interest in a wide dissemination of creative works and to protect free speech. The fair use exceptions help to meet "the need to make each person's addition to the sum of human art and knowledge available for the use of all" (Strong 136). Like many of the other treatments of copyrighted materials, the fair use exception is based on a set of situational criteria rather than on set rules or principles.

The fair use exception is the most important treatment of copyright for educators. Not only does it embody a basic principle of education that furthering the development of knowledge is a valuable goal, but it is also the legal exception to copyright upon which educators and librarians, or anyone concerned with furthering knowledge, will most often rely to use materials that help meet educational goals. Fair use supports the principle that the public should have access to knowledge in order to create new knowledge. With this concept rides the implication that the public has an interest in access to all new knowledge in order to enable all individuals to meet their human potential. Although not explicitly stated in the statute, the constitutional goals of egalitarian access to participatory government support the explicitly stated goals of the intellectual property statute to create a public domain from which to draw in order to advance learning.

On a pragmatic level, within the bounds of four criteria, the fair use exceptions allow educators to use copyrighted materials to help them advance the goals of learning. The statute applies these four criteria in a test of whether a use is judged fair or unfair:

1. the purpose and character of the use, including whether such use is of a commercial nature or is for nonprofit educational purposes;
2. the nature of the copyrighted work;
3. the amount and substantiality of the portion used in relation to the work as a whole; and
4. the effect of the use of the potential market for and value of the copyrighted work. (17 U.S.C. sec 107 [1988])

If the purpose and character of the use promote learning or make criticism or parody of another's ideas or expression possible, the fair use exception is usually applicable. Criticism and comment—which includes parody—as well as news reporting, teaching, scholarship, and research, although excepted from violation by fair use, are subject to a court's scrutiny under the four criteria presented above.

Assertion of fair use takes the form of an affirmative defense, which means that if infringement is either established or readily admitted, fair use can still exempt a user from legal liability. Once a court finds that an intellectual product is infringed, it must determine whether the use, nonetheless, falls into a category of protected exemptions. The codification of fair use exceptions, effected in 1978, was intended to restate the established judicial doctrine of fair use, but as with all laws, over time, the statutory intent has been interpreted in application to current intellectual property issues. The statute requires that a fair use exception be applicable in cases in which the use is "productive," "resulting in some added benefit to the public beyond that produced by the first author's work" (Patry 364). Decisions based on productivity of use are often aided by applying another fair use factor: the purpose and character of the use.

Purpose and Character of Use

Most often, excepted fair uses are personal or educational, or make use of copyrighted material for furthering First Amendment goals such as commentary, criticism, or parody. Lon Fuller lists some specific types of fair uses:

- Quotation of excerpts in a review or criticism for purposes of illustration or comment.
- Quotation of short passages in a scholarly or technical work, for illustration or clarification of the author's observation.
- Use in a parody of some of the content of the work parodied.
- Summary of an address or article, with brief quotations, in a news report.
- Reproduction by a library of a portion of a work to replace part of a damaged copy.
- Reproduction by a teacher or student of a small part of a work to illustrate a lesson.
- Reproduction of a work in legislative or judicial proceedings or reports.
- Incidental or fortuitous reproduction, in a newsreel or broadcast, of a work located at the scene of an event being reported. (24)

In most cases, characterizing a use as commercial leads to denying the fair use privilege, although in a very few cases fair use for commercial purposes has been allowed, the courts stating that commerciality of use has no bearing on whether a public or private benefit is derived.[1]

During development of the 1976 Copyright Act, educational lobbies asked for a broad not-for-profit exemption from copyright but were denied on the basis that general fair use exceptions are provided for all kinds of uses for which relative weight should be given on a case-by-case basis (Patry 368–69); therefore, no specific exemption exists in nonprofit use. However, a characterization of the use as nonprofit can carry weight in favor of the fair use exemption because the Supreme Court has created a specific presumption that all commercial use is un-fair[2] but nevertheless has been consistent in supporting the provision of the First Amendment policy of providing public access to information (Patry 369).

Quotation

The most common allowable use of a copyrighted work within fair use is scholarly quotation. All critics, news reporters, and similarly interested individuals may use quotations without infringement of copyright. The question regarding quotations is whether they actually function as quotation or as copy. For example, in *Publications Int'l Ltd. v. Bally Mfg. Corp.*, the author of a book explaining how to win at the Pac-Man computer game used Pac-Man drawings within the text to clarify his instructions. While the court found this use of copies of the Pac-Man images permissible under fair use, it deemed placement of a Pac-Man image on the front cover of the book outside the realm of fair use because it was used for promotional purposes (Strong 137).

If quotations are used too frequently or in too substantial a portion, the fair use exceptions may not protect the user against infringement. Congress intended the fair use exceptions to allow an author to contribute to knowledge by adding to the knowledge base that already exists, and courts must consider context in determining this purpose. If authors quote another's work in order to build a theory or produce commentary that contributes to a new level of understanding, fair use is applicable. Authors may also quote another author's work to build a case for disagreement, which again contributes new knowledge by developing new understanding of the issues in question. All situations in which authors use copyrighted work to support the goals of learning fall within fair use. But a court will not allow an author to hide behind the fair use exception in order to use another author's work because he or she lacks the creativity, skill, or motivation to produce original work and will deny the fair use exception. In addition, a court might find that an author used another's work for purposes beyond those supported by fair use, such as promotion for economic gain. In these cases also, the fair use defense will be discarded. Courts have found that authors who use another's work to "spice up their prose" or to "enliven or improve" their work will not be protected under the fair use exceptions, particularly when the quotations have been previously unpublished.

For example, when an unofficial biographer quoted from J. D. Salinger's unpublished letters, the court found that the defendant could not claim a fair use exception because he used the quotations to add interest to his work rather than for scholarly commentary. Even upon appeal to the Second Circuit Court, the biographer could not convince the court that his paraphrased text was enough to be exempted by fair use, in great part because the paraphrasing was very close to the original. Courts will often allow narrower uses of the fair use exceptions when the materials used are unpublished. However, the First Circuit Court determined that there was a fair use by another unofficial biographer of a work on L. Ron Hubbard, the founder of Scientology, when the biographer quoted from unpublished materials, because his purpose was to "prove a critical point, or to demonstrate a flaw in the subject's character." But the decision was overturned in the Second Circuit, where the argument was not considered compelling and the use was found unfair (Strong 138–39). Clearly, the fair use defense is not absolute but is dependent on circumstance, the effective use of argument, and often the disposition of the adjudicator. William Strong points to the serious nature of the effects of rulings that limit fair use:

> Many in the copyright bar believe that the Second Circuit [in the L. Ron Hubbard case] has gone overboard in its zeal to protect unpublished works. A broad application of the Hubbard ruling could stifle scholarly use of unpublished materials and not as mere embellishment to scholars' prose. One judge from the panel vigorously dissented from this part of the ruling, and we may hope that future cases will limit the scope of it. (139)

Because fear of the possibility of a limiting outcome can dissuade an author from incorporating another's material into a new work, limitation of fair use can actually inhibit the constitutional purpose of the statute in furthering the advancement of knowledge. Although it may be prudent for authors to minimize the amount of quotation they use in new works, the choice of adherence to this policy should be balanced against the constraints of the inhibition of new expression. In practice, authors should continue to make fair use of quotation for critical purposes. It is only by testing the law that limits of fair use can be extended or that courts can make the boundaries of the law clear.

Critical Comment

The fair use exceptions are traditionally granted to criticism and comment, but the quantity of material used must be limited to only that which is necessary for forming a basis for critical comment. Courts do not allow authors to extract and copy a complete work. Citing large portions of work is allowable, however, if the commentator can demonstrate that the copy is specifically for purposes of fair and reasonable criticism. The question then moves into another realm of the copyright law (to be treated later) in regard to the quantity and substantiality of the work used.

Educational Purposes

Now that educators are using the Internet more often both for local and distance learning, determining what kinds of uses are fair in classroom settings in which networked computers are a means of intraclass communication and participation is very difficult. The fair use exceptions for noncommercial educational uses limit use of copyrighted materials to the classroom, but many instructors make specific classroom use of e-mail communication in world-accessible newsgroups and documents on the World Wide Web a basis for teaching. At first glance, Web-accessible materials used in a classroom forum would clearly seem to fall under the fair use exceptions; however, because materials in these electronic forms, by their very nature, are also accessible to readers outside the confines of the classroom, whether the exception would apply remains to be determined. Arguably, an instructor might upload digitized materials to a closed website or a local area e-mail distribution list and still defend such actions on the basis of the fair use exception for classroom use because the isolated materials would not be accessible by other than students in the class. Only courts can provide an absolute answer to whether this use is fair, but on a scale that considers all the elements of fair use, the instructor would most likely not infringe copyright.

Another controversial issue arising from the relatively recent accessibility and use of digitized materials is the question of what constitutes a copy for purposes of meeting the "one copy per student" guideline. One might argue that a post of a copy of a digitized document to an e-mail discussion list constitutes only one copy because it is only posted once, but equally as valid an argument is that the receipt of the copy by each individual on the discussion list constitutes one copy per individual. An even more extreme treatment of what constitutes a copy in terms of digitized materials is the NII's White Paper stance that simply opening a file to view the material in it is an act of making a copy, since uploading digitized material in order to perceive it requires a "copy" of the digital data on file (Samuelson, *Legally Speaking*).

Educators who assign website development projects to students also face difficulty in clarifying for them whether linking other sites to their own is fair use. In a suit still pending, *Ticketmaster v. Microsoft* treats the linking issue in a commercial context in which Ticketmaster, Inc., is suing the Microsoft Corporation for linking to the interior pages of its site (creating "deep links") for profit. Microsoft defends its actions, arguing that linking on the Web is a universal practice and tantamount to its existence; Microsoft claims that Ticketmaster gave an implied license for linking by loading its site to the Web. Complainants in both *Shetland Times v. Wills* (Bond 194–97) and *The Washington Post v. Total News, Inc.*, also brought suit against site developers for deep-linking their sites for profit, but both cases were settled out of court and provide little instruction for creators or users. Only when the courts decide cases like these will educators have instruction on what to tell their students, but even then, they might have to speculate on a potential outcome of a suit brought in an educational, nonprofit context.[3] Clearly, the fair use guidelines in the current copyright statute do not deal adequately with issues that are directly pertinent to digitized information whether in commercial or noncommercial settings, but the principles of fair use are still applicable in the developing law.

Since educational uses can be commercial or noncommercial, in addition to considering whether the use is educational in nature, users must also consider the potential effect on commerciality of the copied material. As mentioned above, the Supreme Court created a presumption in *Sony* that commercial uses of copyrighted material are unfair, and that presumption carries into educational uses as well; thus, it is important to make clear that use of material is for educational purposes in order to examine whether the commerciality of use affects its legality. Because the bulk of the work used and created by educators is not-for-profit in nature, the remainder of this chapter examines educational fair use and focuses on nonprofit educational uses, which at times must be further classified into categories of classroom or extraclassroom use.

As legislative history makes clear in the 1976 House Report, the fair use guidelines for educational use set the minimum, not maximum, standards for use. In the future, other kinds of copying not mentioned in the 1976 act may be permissible. The House did not intend that the stated fair use guidelines limit uses but only provide standards for use. Just as with all other guidelines for fair use like those provided by universities, libraries, publishing organizations, and others, the House Report guidelines are not law and should not be treated as such. They do, however, provide endorsed interpretations of what the law says. The House report guidelines allow for single copying by or for a teacher at his or her individual request to be used for scholarly research or in teaching or preparation for teaching. This copying may include (but not be limited to) a book chapter; an article from a periodical or newspaper; a short story, poem, or essay; or a chart, diagram, drawing, cartoon, or picture from a book, periodical, or newspaper. Instructors may make multiple copies, in the amount of one per student, limited to classroom use.

Duplicating and distributing multiple copies for classroom uses are considered noninfringing if the copying is brief, spontaneous, and has no detrimental cumulative effect on the marketing of the original, and if the reproducer is careful to include copyright notice on each copy (Patry 405). Detailed definitions of *brevity, spontaneity,* and the *cumulative effect test* are provided in the guidelines for noninfringing educational uses. The brevity test points to the need to limit the use of a work to only what is necessary to convey the ideas behind it in a way that adequately represents the author's intentions. The spontaneity test depends on the individual teacher's immediate inspiration to use the work, and thus immediate copying, and states that in this instance, "[t]he inspiration and decision to use the work and the moments of its use for maximum teaching effectiveness are so close in time that it would be unreasonable to expect a timely reply to a request for permission" (from the copyright holder) (406). The cumulative effect test allows copying for only the course for which the copies are made, not more than one work to be copied from the same author at one time, no more than three works from a collection or volume of a periodical, and no more than nine instances of multiple copying for one course during one term. The commonsense basis for this kind of fair use exemption is to allow educators to copy and distribute materials under reasonable circumstances. Where time constraints or difficulties in locating copyright holders in time to get permission for using materials that are important to teaching a particular class would prohibit the instructor from teaching effectively, fair use applies. The exceptions make clear that the instructor is nonetheless required to make the effort to get copyright permission for further copying when prior immediate constraints are lifted. Lack of zeal in getting permissions is no excuse for recurrent use of materials without permission and would not qualify the instructor for the fair use exemption.

Prohibition against using copies to substitute for anthologies or compilations is strict. In addition, copying that substitutes for the purchase of books or workbooks, standardized tests, or answer sheets is not excepted from infringement. Essentially, instructors should not use copying to avoid buying materials that already exist for educational purposes.

Much controversy has arisen over the course packet cases, in which it is argued whether a copy service can copy and compile multiple-copy course packs to be sold to students. The most recent case deciding the issue was the Sixth Circuit Court of Appeals' review of *Princeton University Press v. Michigan Document Services, Inc.*, in which Princeton University Press and others charged that Michigan Document Services infringed its copyright by making multiple copies of excerpts from materials provided by University of Michigan professors, then creating "course packs" to sell to the students for a profit. The defendants defended their actions on the ground that creating and selling the course packs fell under the fair use exception. The Sixth Circuit Court determined and later affirmed that the copying did not meet all the elements of the test for fair use and thus was not excepted from infringement. Although the decision in this case provides a legal basis for claiming that creating course packs for use in the classroom is illegal, instructors should be aware that the law is not static. Even though the Supreme Court denied to review the appeal of this case, future similar copying treated in another case may at some point be deemed legal.

Parody

Another established exception under fair use is that of parody. Parody is not uncommon among academicians' and students' creations; they derive protection under the First Amendment right to freedom of speech, which carries over to support academic freedom. At the base of any educational endeavor is the pursuit of knowledge and understanding through inquiry and criticism of previous thought and expression. It is not uncommon for critical views of previous knowledge to be expressed through parody, which is often useful for generating critical inquiry and furthering educational goals by supporting the freedom to pursue critical thought, thereby advancing knowledge production. In addition, because creators can construct websites that contain well-integrated visual and textual parody that they can publish easily and quickly, the Web has become a popular forum for parody.[4] Visual imitation, creating a similar but differing copy, is necessary for creating visual parody. Without visual imitation there would be no parody, thus, no statement about the subject parodied. For instance, figure 1, a parody of a Calvin Klein Escape perfume advertisement, imitates the style, color scheme, and layout of the actual Escape ads. The parody, however, depicts an image of a young model "escaping" from an implicitly sleazy photographer. The creator makes a play on words as well as visual style to state that the actual business of modeling for Calvin Klein Escape ads may be unsavory and harmful to young models. The creator of figure 2 also relies on visual imitation to make a point. The image of the year 2000 census form is also a nearly exact copy of the original, but the questions on the form are hyperbolic reconstructions of the original. The creator parodying the year 2000 census makes a humorous statement to bring out a perception of the census as racist and intrusive.

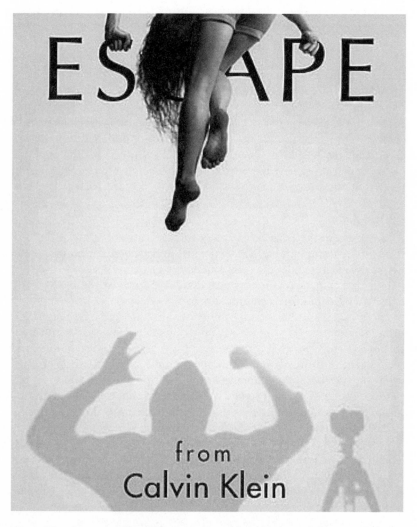

Fig. 1. Visual parody of an Escape perfume advertisement. *Adbusters: Spoof Ads*. 4 April 2000. (http://adbusters.org/spoofads/fashion/escape/)

The difficulty in determining the limits of fair use in parody cases most often lies in how much of the copyrighted work a new author can appropriate for purposes of parody. In general, a parody is considered noninfringing under the fair use exceptions (1) if the creator of the subject of parody is not reasonably expected to parody his or her own

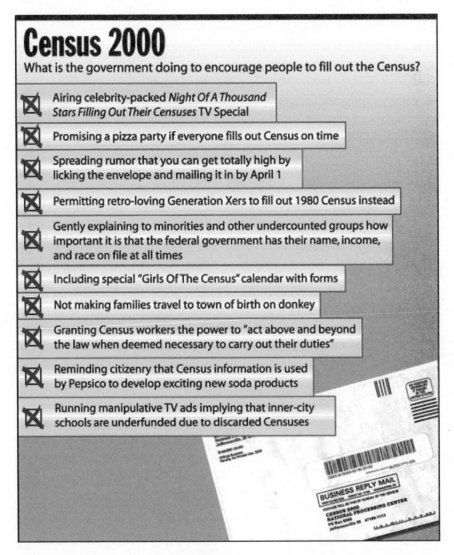

Fig. 2. Political parody of the year 2000 census form. *The Onion.* 4 April 2000. (http://www.theonion.com/onion3610/infograph_3610.html)

material, (2) if the parody is sufficiently unique that it does not fulfill the demand for the original and thus does not compete economically, (3) if the parodist uses the minimal amount of the subject work necessary to create the parodic stance, and (4) if the original is the intended object of the parody (Lindey 11/17).

Courts face difficulty in deciding parody cases because parody, by definition, requires copying original material, so when a court determines copyright infringement based on the existence of substantial similarity, all parody seems to be in violation. The fair use exceptions in the copyright statute except parody from that which courts consider to be infringing.

The 1990 2 Live Crew Supreme Court copyright case, cited above, illustrates the issues that often arise in typical parody cases. When the rap group 2 Live Crew included a version of the Roy Orbison hit "Oh, Pretty Woman" sandwiched between tracks of "Me So Horny" and "My Seven Bizzos," Acuff-Rose, the copyright holder, filed an infringement suit in federal district court in Nashville, Tennessee. The question was not whether the rap group copied some of the lyrics from "Oh, Pretty Woman," but whether their copy was protected parody under fair use. The court found that although the lyrics start out the same as those in the original version, describing a fantasy about a beautiful woman encountered on the street, they develop into those that indicate a very different, contrasting fantasy about a "big hairy woman," "a bald-headed woman," and a "two-timin' woman." Pointing to the work's status as parody, the trial court agreed that 2 Live Crew's rendition of "Oh, Pretty Woman" was noninfringing, partially convinced by testimony from well-known folk singer Oscar Brand that the group's rap lyrics exist to make fun of the white establishment's banal treatment of beauty. The case was appealed to the Sixth Circuit, whose court ruled against 2 Live Crew on the grounds that their version was "too blatantly commercial" to qualify as parody.[5] Other lower court cases have also ruled that parody is fair use: the Second Circuit Court of Appeals, in *Castle Rock Entertainment, Inc. v. Carol Publishing Group, Inc.*, decided that Carol Publishing's *The Seinfeld Aptitude Test,* a trivia quiz book that tested its readers' memories about the television series, *Seinfeld,* was also a fair use because it was parody. Another second circuit court case treated a parody of photographer Annie Leibovitz's photograph of a pregnant Demi Moore, which had been displayed on the cover of *Vanity Fair* magazine. The parody depicted actor Leslie Nielsen's face on a photograph of a nude, pregnant woman in the same stance as that of Demi Moore to advertise Nielsen's movie *Naked Gun 33 1/3.* Even though the Second Circuit Court allowed this depiction as exempted parody, in a case before the Ninth Circuit Court of Appeals, the court held that Penguin Books could not publish a book intended to parody the O. J. Simpson murder trial in the style of Dr. Seuss. The court determined that it was not protected parody under fair use, since potential harm to the Dr. Seuss name overrode the claim to parody. These cases, taken as a whole, instruct educators and other creators that parody is protected under fair use if balanced evenly against the potential for harm to the creator of the work parodied.

Some courts state that to qualify as parody, a work has to be sufficiently similar to the original to conjure up the concept of parody in the receiver's mind, even though it should not follow its subject too closely. More often than not, courts decide this issue on the basis of the economic impact of the parody on the first work. The argument is that the purpose of copyright protection is to ensure that an author benefit from the work and that a parody, by its very nature, would be noncompetitive. "For if a copy does not compete with the original—and it would be a strange parody that competed with its subject—then more leeway ought to be allowed in the quantity of the copying. This is certainly the intent of Congress in adopting its four criteria of fair use" (Strong 141).

Although the issue of the right to free speech seems an obvious basis of argument for parody cases, the fair use exceptions are based not in the First Amendment but in the copyright statute. First Amendment arguments can always be brought separately in court, although precedent shows that they are not often successful (142). Notwithstanding the lack of "explicit connection between free speech and fair use exceptions," the force of free speech concepts influence the granting of fair use exceptions nonetheless.[6]

Harry N. Rosenfield argues in "The American Constitution, Free Inquiry, and the Law," that in cases in which the copyright clause and the First Amendment conflict, the First Amendment takes primacy. He points out that the First Amendment does not mitigate restrictions of the copyright law but that it provides additional assurance that the public can maintain access to information. As he explains, "'fair use' and the First Amendment are separate and distinguishable protections for users of copyrighted materials" (291). Where fair use provides access to copyrighted materials as long as the work's marketability is not impaired, the First Amendment may be applied despite the fact that marketability is impaired because "public communication of public information is too important to the welfare of a free and democratic society to be subjected to the private monopoly provided by the current concept of copyright" (L. Ray Patterson 1211).

Two different Second Circuit panels of judges have specifically noted that they based their holdings on a view toward First Amendment freedoms and their impact on copyright.[7] The Court in *Consumers* noted that fair use codified the judicial law's basis in ensuring the dissemination of information (Patry 461). Copyright developed directly from a desire to protect the right to information:

> [C]opyright in the United States was *not* born from the "interstices" of censorship, but to the contrary, out of fervently held beliefs that freedom of expression could flourish only when it was not subject to government control and that the system of private ownership of property represented the best possible mechanism for providing the citizenry with the security necessary to accomplish that lofty goal. (462)

The fair use provisions are in place to ensure that courts support the focus of copyright on free speech and free dissemination of information. Where the provisions themselves fail to meet that goal, First Amendment arguments are available to provide further assurances. Academicians, in particular, use free speech support as a basis for critical inquiry and both they and their students depend on free speech protections to conduct the processes of education. Without access to the information upon which criticism is based, educators, students, and the general citizenry would not have the capacity to generate free speech at all.

News Reporting

Copyright infringement claims have often been defended by reliance on fair use for news reporting because it is listed as a possible fair use in section 107. News reporting is not often presumed to be a fair use; thus, more often than not, use of the defense is unsuccessful. The courts base their denial of fair use for news reporting on three principal reasons: "(1) lack of a productive use of the copyrighted work; (2) appropriation of the essence or substantial portions of the copyrighted work; and (3) the presence of bad faith on the defendant's part" (Patry 410). Cases in which news reporters have been denied the fair use defense include those in which a defendant copied verbatim 92 percent of the plaintiff's article *(Quinto v. Legal Times of Washington, Inc.)*, another abstracted financial news analyses in which the use was considered substantial in quality and quantity *(Wainright Securities, Inc. v. Wall Street Transcript Corp.)*, and another copied a substantial portion of a plaintiff's dissertation, *The Social Psychology of Romantic Love,* as a quiz for entertainment of the defendant's readers *(Rubin v. Boston Magazine Co.)* (411).

News reporting must meet the standards for any other test of fair use and may not infringe a copyright by exceeding the limits of what courts consider fair; however, like parody, where reporters attempt to justify copying through copyright claims of fair use and fail, they may use First Amendment reasoning to justify acts that could be considered copyright infringement. For instance, where some courts have considered that copying a substantial quantity of material is copyright infringement and they discover a commercial or bad faith intent, in instances when reporters use a substantial amount of material that sheds light on political graft or other wrongdoing, the same courts are more likely to protect the use in support of First Amendment goals.

Nature of the Work

Where the use of a work is important in determining whether that use is fair, and despite the hesitance to create a presumptive protection in certain classes of works, the statute also shows that the nature of a work is significant to courts when they make fair use determinations. Although the statute specifically treats sections other than those listed below, these are most pertinent to the needs and interests of educators in humanities fields; thus the omission here of treatment of architectural plans, biographies and historical works, maps, and others.

Collections and Anthologies

Academicians may wish to create an anthology of works authored by individual researchers. Unless specific contract arrangements between the publisher/compiler and the author have been made, collections contain works in which there are two copyright interests: a copyright grant to the publisher/compiler of the work and a grant to the author. The details of each copyright holder's rights will be specific to the agreement between the holder and the publisher/compiler and will be different from collection to collection. In addition, the copyright in each individual work is distinct from the copyright in the work as a whole (Patry 419). The guidelines for educational fair use, specified in the 1976 House Report, apply to collections in the same way that they do to other copyrighted work. The difference in cases regarding collections or anthologies is that most writers of work used in anthologies are paid a separate fee for each time they license their work because the likelihood of the publication of their collected works is low. The courts take this special situation into consideration when deciding copyright cases whose subject is collections and tend to grant stronger protection against infringement of works in collections.

Video and Audio Productions

Multimedia production, a quickly expanding category of creation, often requires using copyrighted video and audio clips; thus, it is likely that creators will use them in developing multimedia work or will need to be aware of the protections available for their own video and audio productions. Infringement in video and audio productions, unlike that in text, can occur in display and performance as well as in copying. "'[D]isplay' is defined as the nonsequential showing of individual images of the work, whereas to 'perform' such a work is to 'show its images in any sequence or to make the sounds accompanying it audible'" (Patry 423). While legislative reports indicate that fair use exceptions should be very narrowly allowed in displaying and performing video and audio productions, they note that excerpts from performances are still protected use for the purposes of criticism and comment (H.R. Rept. 94–1476, 94th Cong., 2d sess. 72–73 [1976]; Sen. Rept. 94–473, 94th Cong., 1st sess. 65 [1975]).

Often courts look to public interest beyond the value of entertainment in the dissemination of video and audio productions to determine whether a fair use exception is applicable. In these cases, courts tend to focus on the economic impacts of use of the work rather than the actual nature of the work itself. It cannot be denied, however, that a work's economic value is inherent in its nature; thus, a court's consideration of these issues in conjunction is proper and expected.

Compilations

Argument often arises around application of the copyright law to compilations because factual data, the basis of compilations, is not protected under the law, but the expression created by compiling the facts that make up the content is. Determining the fair use question is even more problematic, since the potential outcome of a decision on the basic infringement question is unclear (Patry 426). A creator may gain protection in compilations if arrangement of the materials is unique enough to result in an original work but, as with all other copyright protection, only the arrangement is protected. A court will not grant copyright protection simply because the process of compilation was difficult, a large economic investment was required, and the value of the resulting work was high, although the question of value and investment is important in fair use determinations. As mentioned earlier, fair use is an affirmative defense and a separate issue from the determination of infringement itself. Regardless, courts often confuse the issues and deny fair use exceptions even when infringement might not be demonstrated (427).

Workbooks, Standardized Test Sheets, Exercises, and Similar Materials

Another category of protected works includes standardized tests, workbooks, and fill-in-the-blank worksheets, called "consumables." The 1976 House Report guidelines indicate that these materials are not protected under fair use. The obvious need for this prohibition is that these materials exist only for purposes of teaching, and value in their development and protection easily could be destroyed if copying were allowed. In the case of standardized admission tests such as the SAT, LSAT, GRE, and MEDCAT, even more stringent protection is needed to ensure that unfair preparation or cheating is prohibited.

Out-of-Print and Unpublished Works

Although some argue that the fair use exception for unpublished works is available through the federal statute, in general, the states apply the common law and deem it prohibited. The legislative history of the 1976 act indicates that it was the intent of Congress to continue the common law prohibition against fair use of unpublished works but also makes clear that if the work is performed or voluntarily disseminated by the author, fair use should be allowed (Patry 441–42). Congress did explicitly provide for reproduction of unpublished works such as dissertations to preserve the work and to allow research.

Amount and Substantiality of the Portion of a Work Used

While substantiality and amount of the work used are factors in determining whether infringement of a copyrighted work has occurred, they are also among the determinants of whether the fair use exception is applicable. As discussed above, the guidelines for fair use in not-for-profit classroom use indicate that instructors can legally copy a whole short story, poem, essay, song, and article under specific circumstances. Fair use also allows individuals to videotape entire programs from television for personal use. But courts may not allow an instructor to copy entire works if a description of the contextual situation demonstrates that he or she failed to meet the limitations of immediacy and inspiration described above. Substantiality and amount of the work used may also be a factor in deciding whether the effect of the copying is harmful to the potential market value of the work. A copy may be substantial enough to substitute for the work and to discourage what would otherwise result in the sale of that work. In this case, courts will weigh the benefit of the copying against the negative effect upon the market value of the work.

Potential Market Value of the Work and the Effect of Use

In order to defeat a fair use exception, a plaintiff must show that economic injury has occurred (on the basis of the harmful effect of the use of the work on the potential market value of the work) (Patry 454). The Supreme Court created a bifurcated test for fair use based on whether the use was commercial or noncommercial in *Sony Corp. v. Universal Studios, Inc.* "[T]he Court held that 'every commercial use of copyrighted material is presumptively an unfair exploitation of the monopoly privilege that belongs to the owner of copyright'" (454), but for noncommercial uses the Court applied a more complicated test. The test of fair use in noncommercial uses provides that after meeting all the requirements of the fair use provisions, the use must still not impair the marketability of the work to the extent that it is likely to cause future harm. The difficulty lies in determining the meaning of "the likelihood of future harm" (455). In developing the laws, some legislators argued that a use that diminishes the possibility of sales of the work in future markets is enough, whereas others, particularly those who support educators, asserted that the application of this test would be so broad that it would harm the public's interest in accessing information (H.R. Rept. 2237, 89th Cong., sess. 64 [1966]). As with all intellectual property cases, the effect that copying a work has on its potential marketability differs from one situational context to another.

In the same way that courts must decide issues regarding fair use within frameworks of context, the rules of law regarding intellectual property are affected by both technology and societal interpretation. The following chapter analyzes the effect of technology and interpretation on the intellectual property law.

4

Law and Policy:
The Balance in Cyberspace

The rules of law, like the structures of the legal system, are intricate, sometimes complicated, and often difficult to interpret. The Internet's networked communication and the digitization of text make it even more complicated for courts to interpret the law because digitized text has characteristics to which the 1976 statute does not speak directly; thus, issues that arise as a result of the use of digitized text are yet unsettled. For instance, because copyright protection ensues for a work that is "fixed" in a "tangible" form, characterizations of what constitutes "fixity" and "tangibility" in regard to digitized text must be clear. In addition, when educators use the Internet as the locus of classroom participation, which can make classroom material accessible worldwide, particularly in distance learning classes, they face complications in determining whether the uploading of works for classroom use is protected under fair use. In fact, simply defining *classroom* is difficult when the locus for class participation in distance learning forums in is "cyberspace."

Since the current statutory law fails to reflect the changes that using new technology brings, it is important that academicians who make use of technology in their classrooms be involved in affecting the law that will impact their work. Statutes are created in both state and federal courts, but the copyright statute, federally promulgated and given power for enactment by the Constitution, overrides the state statutes. The power to enact federally binding intellectual property law is stated in Article 1, section 8 of the Constitution, which provides Congress with authorization to create laws that give "authors and inventors the exclusive right to their respective writings and discoveries" subject to limitations by the public's right of access.

The courts can also make law by enforcing and interpreting the statutes, invalidating the statutes, or creating new law on the basis of common law. The 1976 Copyright Act provides a copyright holder with a limited exclusive right to protect the work from infringement; where a court determines that the right lies with the plaintiff, it can enforce the statute against the infringing party. Courts can also create law in areas not covered by the statutes, the "common law" subject areas. For example, the law fails to speak to whether a creator can use copyright to protect an expression specifically because it is personal or private, so the courts have created laws in the rights to publicity and privacy under common law in order to remedy situations not directly treated in the statute. When precedential directives of the court become well established, the legislature commonly eventually introduces them as a bill and codifies them in order to provide clear statutory law.

Courts may also make law by interpreting the statutes while deciding court cases. Particularly in light of the current statute, which provides no specific language regarding treatment of digital communication, this interpretation is important. For example, as mentioned above, the statute does not explain the meanings of fixity and tangibility as they relate to digitized communication; thus, it is the courts' job to do so. Interpretation is difficult in cases that require knowledge in specialized areas of information like that involved in the Internet; lawyers and judges are often not aware of the special contextual circumstances that surround the needs for use of technology and develop technical rather than practical understanding, which can lead to highly detrimental interpretations of the law. For instance, when courts apply strictly technological definitions to determine the parameters of fixity, they may find that a digital document is not only fixed but also copied as soon as it becomes visible in a computer system. The result would mean that merely viewing digital work could be considered a violation of copyright; thus, the strict technological interpretation, without context, could lead to a chilling effect on the dissemination of digital information. Therefore, lawyers and judges must pursue cases involving digital technology with a complete contextual as well as textual understanding of the impact of their interpretations in order to make law that is valid. Educators and other individuals with particular interests in affecting the developing intellectual law as it relates to technology can help to educate legislators, lawyers, and judges by participating in organizations with this purpose, as well as by developing contacts with local bar associations and political organizations in order to pursue these educational purposes.

In addition, all individuals participate in creating intellectual property laws by virtue of participating in society. One form of direct participation is in becoming a litigant in an intellectual property suit. But in 1998, the No Electronic Theft (NET) Act was passed and signed into law, making it possible to charge and convict a violator of copyright under criminal law, which inhibits users from pursuing their rightful use of copyrighted materials. No case has yet been brought under the NET Act, and it is unlikely that a criminal case would be brought except under extreme circumstances. Intellectual property suits are primarily civil rather than criminal cases, initiated when one individual or organization files a complaint against another, claiming that it copied or used its intellectual product. Legal process can be intimidating and can create a barrier of fear that inhibits individuals' assertion of their constitutionally stated rights in use of intellectual products. But new law is created and old law is clarified by individuals' participation in legal processes. In fact, all individuals do participate in the process, either by testing the issues in order to establish answers for what is allowable fair use of materials in classroom settings or by remaining silent out of fear or apathy and thus creating a presumption of acquiescence with the development of law as it is.

Many of the organizational and university intellectual property guidelines and copyright notices in websites and print materials are overrestrictive, also contributing to the perception that using copyrighted materials at all is prohibited. But these guidelines are not law; they are only interpretations of the law. In addition, when they indicate that copyrighted materials are absolutely restricted from use, they are inaccurate and misleading. Fair use makes the policy intent of public access explicit and provides specific language framing uses that are not restricted by the copyright law. Despite their fears, users should know that they are legally empowered to use copyrighted materials within the parameters of fair use.

Educators and individual users may be fearful that their actions in using intellectual products could lead to costly litigation. At present, the looming presumption regarding intellectual property rights is that the copyright holder maintains the strongest grant of protection from the statute. This presumption is bolstered by protectionist-oriented lawyers who tout the strong protection of rights in authors and inventors but fail to mention the constitutionally based limitations on those rights.[1] Materials provided to "help" the nonlawyer "understand" intellectual property law often do the same. An example of the typical protectionist-based information is the Cyber-law offering, available on-line for free and touted as a short course in intellectual property issues. This material is provided on-line, intended as a primer for nonlawyers who have an interest in learning about intellectual property issues. To receive this information, the participant must simply subscribe to the Cyber-law list.[2] Two or three times a month the participant receives an e-mail message that "explains" an aspect of the intellectual property law in simple, non-legal, and nondetailed language. The Cyber-law subscription allows no discussion and no way to send responses and criticism of the posted material to other receivers of the Cyber-law "course." The information provided is protectionist-oriented. In failing to provide detail, even if for the sake of simplifying the information for nonlawyers, it omits references to statements in the statutes that support users' rights to copyrighted materials.

In addition, broad statements that take a strong stance for protecting authors' rights are common to the legal handbooks or primers that are available for nonlawyer creators who want to know how to protect their work from abuse by others. Handbook writers focus on protecting the interests of authors in part because the purposes and interests of readers who buy handbooks are in knowing how the laws will protect their interests in authorship; books that help meet these readers' needs sell more readily. In fact, there is an element of wisdom in providing defensive rather than offensive information. In other words, authors who provide material that explains how to protect information are not likely to be responsible if a user sues for rights to access, provided that the information included in the treatise is a correct listing of the statutory law as stated. If, on the other hand, a handbook writer provides a treatise on how to pursue a right to use another's work, particularly because fair use is so contextually situated that the results vary from case to case, the risk is high that a writer would provide information that could embroil a reader in heavy legal processes.

Introduction of the Internet into everyday commerce has caused a protectionist trend among law professionals. Lawyers are scrambling for ways to protect their clients' interests in an age where technology makes it easier than ever before to violate copyright holders' rights. Digitization not only makes it easy to copy material quickly and exactly, but it allows a breadth of copy and transfer in mere minutes that was never before possible. Most books for nonlawyers are written for readers who want to create and use material for commercial markets, and many share these fears about protecting their intellectual products. These handbooks appropriately address this audience's interests.

In addition, the great majority of intellectual property lawyers are hired by clients such as authors, film producers, musicians, and software producers whose interest is in protecting their work. Most of the defense work done by intellectual property lawyers occurs in situations in which cases turn on disputes over copyright, trademark, or patent ownership;

contract agreements; or establishment of work for hire relationships. It is natural that these lawyers, as writers, would pursue the same protectionist stances that drive their everyday work; this is the information they know well and that will, to their minds, benefit their readers most.

The forgotten, nonrepresented party with an interest in intellectual property law is the public, made up of the individual, the student, the critic, the journalist, the librarian, the scholar, and in essence, the American culture, all with a need to access information in order to obtain and to contribute to the knowledge that drives the country. The Internet makes access to information even more important than ever before. The very ease of copy and dissemination of information that causes fear in lawyers whose duty is to protect their clients' work is also what makes access to that information so important. The Internet is becoming our greatest source of unrestricted news and information. Print publishers go through lengthy screening processes to decide what will be printed for public consumption. Their decisions are based on marketing demands and quality, and are influenced, in part, by a network of mutual support among potential authors and reviewers. In contrast, the Internet makes it possible for anyone with a computer and modem to publish information to be judged by a public readership. The ability to copy and use digital materials as a basis of critique of these unscreened materials is essential to judging the worth of what is digitally published. Alternately, valuable information that might not pass the screening process attached to print publishing may still be published on the Internet. It is also essential that the Internet audience have access to this information in order to lend critical support.

The framers of the Constitution made clear that the right to public access was primary in the copyright clause, but ironically, the benefactors of its protection are in the weakest legal position. Where highly paid lawyers and lobbyists represent commercial, and often corporate, copyright holders, the public has no representation or organizational body to support its interests. Most often, "the public," for legal purposes, takes the form of one kind of individual party or another, and in the case of the great majority of individuals who play the role of David against the commercial Goliath, these individuals are fearful of the foreboding legal structures incumbent with the threat of years of legal conflict and time lost at best and of bankruptcy at worst. The result is that individual users of public information are inhibited in the use of their constitutionally provided protections; the constitutional protection intended by the framers is defeated through an *in terrorem* effect of overzealous protectionists.

Academicians, in particular, should be aware of their influence in interpreting established law. Those who use technology as a basis of teaching and research, especially, should contribute to the development of new law through their actions in dealing with intellectual creations, for academicians have a special interest in fair use as a means of furthering the constitutional goal of the advancement of knowledge. That educators teach classes over networked computers on-site or in distance learning forums should not inhibit their rights of access granted in the copyright statute. In addition, by virtue of their characterization as educators, they maintain special legal status as parties who can make use of the rights granted in the fair use provisions. As such, academicians have a responsibility to maintain the rights provided in the statute by using them as well as by testing them, particularly in new technology-enhanced learning forums.

Academicians who are unsure of the extent of their rights supported by fair use and who fear the threat of legal sanction often want solid guidelines for determining which educational uses of materials are legally allowable. But as I discuss in Part Two, the law is never static and the only way to be sure of the extent of the rights provided is to contribute to their development through the legislative process, then to test them in the courts. The process of contributing to the development of law can be arduous. It requires diligence in keeping abreast of the current law and in maintaining contact with representatives in order to influence the law-making process. Moreover, courage is required of individuals who are not educated in the legal system and who must speak out for the rights of underrepresented individuals against parties often supported by powerful legal representatives with important business associations at the bar and years of experience in the law.

Educators can fight the *in terrorem* effect of hard-line protectionist stances by merely availing the grants of use provided in the statute. Academicians should make attempts to follow the law as stated and not shy away from their granted rights out of fear of the threat of a lawsuit. In the great majority of situations, the copyright holder has little interest in the kinds of uses made by educators. Copyright holders are most concerned with unfair uses by competitors or individuals whose positions as users make them, rather than the copyright holder, the economic benefactors of the use.

Most often in cases where an educator mistakenly infringes a copyright that is not excepted by the fair use provisions and the copyright holder takes notice, the offended party simply sends a letter that asks the user to stop his or her infringing use. If the user finds that his or her use is not excepted by the fair use provisions, the remedy is to stop. Where the user does not agree, negotiation can ensue. It is often not until negotiation fails that a plaintiff actually files an infringement claim and that the process of civil suit begins; thus, there is little to fear in the every-day cases of use and conflict.

In particular, in areas where the law is undeveloped like that in Internet cases, it is very important to test the potential boundaries. It is difficult to establish a law if it would require behavior that is contrary to everyday practice. As I explain in detail in Part Two, a shift in societal perceptions and cultural mores can effect a change in everyday practice, and over time, an established law can become a blue law and be ignored to such an extent that it is effectively abolished. Participants who are knowledgeable about the technological effects and the social impact of the new technology could offer valuable guidance to legislators and lawyers who may not be experienced in the communal structure of cyberspace interaction. Educators who use and study networked communication could offer a particularly broad wealth of information and insight because these are the individuals who have struggled to understand the political, educational, and economic effects of the Internet and digitized information since their inception. Nonlegal expertise in dealing with cyberspace law is as important as legal expertise.

Academic humanists are interested in using technology for furthering knowledge and support egalitarian access and contribution to the development of the character of the nation. We all contribute to the public consciousness either through action or inaction, but we contribute nevertheless. Our contribution should be well considered, purposeful, and when necessary, courageous. Understanding the effects of culture and community on societal decisions can help to clarify the roles we play as participants in our respective professional fields. Chapter 5 analyzes these effects so that conclusions may be applied to issues in intellectual property.

Part Two

Ideology and Power

5

Controlling Construction: The Internet, Law, and Humanistic Studies

Society's cultural influences help to create us as a people and a nation; no individual or community develops in isolation. Communities' values, beliefs, and goals shape the development of organizational structures, and their ideologies drive community actions. Despite the fact that law is a system of rules, that humanistic studies are academic disciplines, and that the Internet is a technological system, each is also an organization of people who are influenced by the values, beliefs, and goals of other members of their organization. In other words, regardless of the fact that each individual has a separate and distinct identity, may maintain viewpoints that conflict with those of others in the community, and may also be a member of other communities, each community is made up of individuals who are drawn together in a framework of culture. It is important to understand the cultural drives behind each of these communities, particularly as they influence ideology, in order to examine how issues in intellectual property both affect and are affected by community forces. In fact, when intellectual property law is interpreted from an ideology that supports protection of individual economic interest over that of the public in information and knowledge creation, it can hamper a community's ability to determine its own culture as well as its future. Individuals from communities driven by ideologies contrary to those that would support a protectionist stance should understand the cultural effect of ideology in order to participate in influencing it in a way that represents their alternate voices. The law has power to affect culture and community:

... [T]he law operates hegemonically—it is at work shaping social worlds of meaning—not only when it is institutionally encountered, but when it is consciously and unconsciously apprehended.
Hegemonic power is operative when threats of legal action are
made as well as when they actually acted upon. (Coombe, *Cultural
Life* 9)

In *The Cultural Life of Intellectual Properties: Authorship, Appropriation, and the Law,* Rosemary Coombe approaches trademark law
from the standpoint of cultural anthropology and examines it specifically and in great detail, showing that a cultural studies approach to
intellectual property is important for understanding the effects of culture and community on trademarks and vice versa. When we distinguish
the cultural characteristics of each of the three communities—academic
humanists, the Internet, and the law—it becomes clear that although
each is driven by differing societal forces, each is also socially constructed
and, therefore, subject to individual and cultural influences that ultimately affect views of and influences on intellectual property law. We
must examine society's cultural frameworks to understand the operation of law and the actions within a community regarding it. And examination reveals that dissonance and conflict are necessary for developing negotiated consensus that is, ideally, representative of the whole
of the community. Individuals in the legal and humanistic studies communities are drawn together through interests in common work-related
topics, but just as educators in humanistic studies and law professionals do, Internet participants exhibit behaviors consistent with those that
indicate the existence of community, even though they may also be
members of other communities. The Internet community is socially constructed to the extent that its actions and attitudes toward information
indicate common patterns of shared values. The legal community is
somewhat complex in that its members are organized functionally to interpret and apply the law as a framework of rules, but as a community
it is also an organization of individuals who either share or are driven
by a dominant ideology. Examining the effect of shared culture and ideology within individual communities shows that a community's cultural
and ideological drives are created through a dialogic process of communal negotiation. This points to the function and importance of participatory democracy in developing intellectual property law; this
chapter's examination of culture and ideology within these three communities is helpful in understanding why public access to knowledge and
its process of creation are essential to us all.

Just as fundamental to understanding the effects of the law on communities, cultures, and their converse is a clear conception of the role

that ideology plays in constructing community and culture and in affecting law. Definitions of the terms *ideology, community,* and *culture* make clear their integrative nature. Notwithstanding definitions related to locale, community is also "a group or class having common interests," "similarity or identity: a community of interests," and "society as a whole: the public" (299). Culture is both "the totality of socially transmitted behavior patterns, arts, beliefs, institutions, and all other products of human work and thought characteristic of a community or population" and "a style of social and artistic expression peculiar to a society or class" (348), and ideology is defined as "the body of ideas reflecting the social needs and aspirations of an individual, group, class, or culture" (639). These definitions evidence the essential nature of intellectual expression as a socially binding element, as well as a fundamental reflection of the internal drives of individuals and groups. One legal scholar notes that

> what unites the ideas of culture, personhood, and historical evidence is information. To be a part of culture, to be socialized or acculturated, is to posses a certain kind of information—cultural know-how. Cultures are populations of individuals with relatively similar kinds of cultural information. To be a person is to be constituted by a particular kind of cultural information that exists at a particular point in time. The cultural information within human beings grows, changes, and evolves as we come in contact with others. It is reflected in our technology, in our institutions, and in the articulation of values we hold most dear. (Balkin ix)

Clearly, information in the form of intellectual expression is a binding force among individuals constituted within community associations. Ideology supports the social collection of individuals by encompassing "the socially generated and socially sustained ways in which human beings understand and constitute their world" (2). It is the "language of the purposes of a social group" (Harris 22). Cultural and social anthropologist Clifford Geertz uses these defining principles to understand the interplay among ideology, community, and culture: (1) social interaction continually creates and recreates culture—people create their own culture rather than it being imposed on them, (2) culture has no deterministic power to create and it cannot be created by some external power such as law, and (3) culture exists only to the extent that its participants perceive that it does ("Thick Description" 12–13, 26–27). People create their own cultures and communities, driven by common ideologies that help bind them together, and intellectual expression, the embodiment of culture, is the very essence that can bind individuals into communities based on shared ideologies and that also enables them to effect change and redirect ideology and thus, culture. The intellectual property law that results from these influences also further influences newly developing culture:

> Legal regimes of intellectual property shape (although they do not determine) the ways in which cultural signs are re/appropriated by those who assert difference in the spaces of similarity, imitating and mimicking signs of authority to express relations of alterity. . . . [I]ntellectual property law does not function simply in a rule-like fashion, nor is it adequately portrayed as a regime of rights and obligations. Although it is constructed through a rhetoric of rights, . . . it is also simultaneously a generative condition and a prohibitive boundary for hegemonic articulation and subaltern practices of appropriation. (Coombe, *Cultural Life* 27)

Law simultaneously affects and reflects culture. What is most important is that the culture that the law represents is often one with power to affect a culture of lesser strength, and that is the basis for my examination of community, culture, and ideology as it influences and is influenced by intellectual property law. Ideology is a combination of dominant thought and power. Community ideology reflects an intermingling of the most dominant thought of an association of minds and the power with which that thought is imbued; thus, efforts to understand the makeup of communities and the dominant ideologies that drive and represent them are essential.

A dominant ideology has the power to affect law and culture and its converse; however, powerful ideological dominance in a community is by no means either static or demands that all individuals in the community conform to one governing pattern of thought:

> The nature of the group which provides the basis for the ideology—which makes it an 'ideology' rather than an individual's eccentric philosophy—arises from any of an infinite number of influences. . . . But what is true of a social group may not be true of its individual members . . . [since] each individual participates only in certain fragments of the group "thought-system," the totality of which is not in the least a mere sum of these fragmentary individual experiences. (Harris 42–43)

In fact, dissonance within a community creates the space for the change, growth, and development of thought that is necessary to meet the demands that increased and improved knowledge makes on people within a society. In the same way that individuals can be members of a community without subscribing to each aspect of that community's dominant ideologies, an individual also can share simultaneous membership in more than one community. Although seemingly contradictory, people may carry a cultural tradition from one community with them long after moving into a new community with new traditions. American constitutional lawyers disagree on meanings of the Constitution while they are also part of the same constitutional tradition (Balkin 8–9).

Situating the framing parameters that establish communal associations of individuals and locating the ideological sources of power around which those communities are organized can reveal the potential impact of ideological power on society and the nation at large. By examining the bases of culture from which the humanistic academic, Internet, and legal communities arise and by locating their dominant ideologies, we can assess the potential effect of their different ideologies on how each would interpret intellectual property law. It becomes clear then, why the ideological basis upon which intellectual property law is interpreted and developed should be one that represents an even cross section of all members of our national society.

Constructing Knowledge and Power

Since the 1970s, humanists have embraced the belief that communities of academicians, workplace writers, and researchers are socially constructed. Social construction tells us that we create reality through communicative language, that we are socially bound by the ideas that the community supports, and that there is no external "Truth" or foundation that exists outside what the community has established through language. In fact, social theorists in humanistic studies note that reality is unknowable apart from language (Blyler and Thralls 3). Social construction actually extends the concept that groups may share a common language and linguistic terms and markers in a way that leads to shared understanding as a group, a discourse community. Where a discourse community is made up of a group of individuals who communicate through the same language patterns and vocabulary that are specific and unique to the community, a socially constructed community is pulled together under the same paradigmatic framework of thought, agrees on similar societal values and goals, and shares the same fundamental beliefs in a transitive basis of acceptance that functions to serve community purposes until the conviction shifts. Just as individuals become a part of discourse communities by sharing common vocabulary definitions and sentence patterns, they become a part of a social construct by defining *themselves,* either what they are or are not, through the paradigm of the community.

"An individual is not born as a member of society but only with a predisposition for sociality" (Berger and Luckman 129), but community is central to social construction (Blyler and Thralls 7). The individual assimilates into a community by becoming a part of the discourse community, then developing an understanding, and for most, acceptance of the dominant paradigms of that community. When individuals internalize the social construct, they are then members of society (Berger and Luckman 130). To assimilate into a community and to become a part of the social construct of that community, individuals must mesh their identities with that of the community of which they want to become a part. "What is most important for our consideration here is the fact that the individual not only takes on the roles and attitudes of others, but in the same process takes on their world" (132). What may at first glance seem like a process involving forceful compliance is not that at all. Individuality is not lost, but individuals with like paradigms of thought find others with whom to share common societal interests and goals and, in doing so, define their own identities as they compare themselves to what are often diverse members of the same community. "To be given identity involves being assigned a specific place in the world" (132).

This is not to say, however, that assimilation into one community is mutually exclusive of membership in another. Multiple communal memberships are so much a part of everyday life that we rarely consider them. Most people maintain simultaneous membership in workplace communities, neighborhood communities, families, and recreational communities. Each community has a specific expectation regarding what is considered appropriate language and demeanor, and participants adjust, often without noticing. In fact, many members of the legal community participate on the Internet and are a part of that community as well and these memberships are not mutually exclusive. But these individuals adjust their actions when they move from community to community, following the dominant ideological constructs of each. For example, as noted above, even protectionist-oriented law professionals copy others' materials into their posts when discussing issues on e-mail lists. The Internet community's ideological construct not only supports this activity but reflects an operating structure of sharing information that is essential to its very embodiment. Individuals cannot become participants in the Internet community without accepting this basis for sharing information.

Participants in the Internet community often influence educators who use the Internet as a teaching forum, and these coparticipants often share ideological values. Educators in humanistic fields have used networked computers in classroom forums to support classroom instruction that is fundamentally dialogic in nature (Hawisher et al.), and the role technology plays in both social construction and support of networked communication among students and instructors is to aid the creation of knowledge in the humanities. Through networked communication, students are better able to participate in developing the community of the classroom, and the instructor becomes a participant in social construction rather than a dominant authoritative voice (Barrett 107). The constructed Internet culture is established in much the same way. Generat-

ing community through technological systems is just as possible as doing so in academic disciplines; the descriptive quality of community
applies to both systems, which are created by and of people:

> The fact that community has some sort of descriptive meaning can-
> not really be doubted. That is to say it is not used in a *wholly* evalu-
> ative way, but having said this the range of its descriptive meaning
> is very wide, and indeed some features which have been held to be
> definitive of community by different theorists may well be incom-
> patible. Community has been linked to locality, to identity of func-
> tional interests, to a sense of belonging, to shared cultural and eth-
> nic ideas and values, to a way of life opposed to the organization
> and bureaucracy of modern mass society, etc.—a whole nexus of
> traits some of which may well turn out, on analysis, to be incom-
> patible. (Plant 13)

The very concept of community is complicated and abstract. "Community is both empirically descriptive of a social structure and normatively
toned. It refers both to the unit of society as it is and to the aspects of
that unit that are valued if they exist and are desired in their absence"
(Minar and Geer 13). What is of great significance for the Internet community is the ability to use a powerful tool for connectivity in the form
of the computer-linking network. "All interaction within a community
takes place within a web of inclusive ties" (16), and there has never been
a technology with more power to create communal ties. The efficiency
of the Internet for enabling conversations among individuals with like
concerns, even when their approaches to those concerns may cause conversations to heighten in conflict, if not enthusiasm, makes it a perfect
medium for reifying emergent communities, bypassing any requirement
for physical proximity. The general history of the Internet is well known
to most, but what is most significant is that although it began as
ARPANET, a means to simply transfer defense-related data from one
place to another, its evolution into the system we know now arose because participants on the early form of the Internet converged around
social concerns. Although users originally confined their posts to work-
based communications, as the use of e-mail grew, they began to become
more relaxed with what they communicated. "Not only was the network
expanding, it was opening wider to new uses and creating new connections among people" (Hafner and Lyon 205). By 1975, computer researchers from a variety of fields began to use ARPANET. "Access to
the Net was still limited . . . but the diversity of users at those sites was
nonetheless creating a community of users distinct from the engineers
and computer scientists who built the ARPANET" (229). Eventually, the
government provided funding for the communication system and, on the
basis of the term *Internet Protocol,* named the public-funded system the

"Internet" (244). As more university-based academicians gained access to ARPANET and eventually the Internet, the system developed into what it is today, a connecting point for ideas from diverse individuals from all over the world.

A growing number of individuals have become linked and active in Internet communication, and the Internet has developed markers of community as well as its own culture, often called the "Net Culture." Membership in the Net Culture does not require like-mindedness in all things; racist "hate sites" exist alongside sites that support diversity and undiluted multicultural acceptance. Instead, community develops from shared experience that is made apparent by common language characteristics. As social constructionists Bruffee, Berger and Luckman, and others point out, a shared reality among individuals is developed through linguistic communication. With the development of the World Wide Web as a subcategory of the Internet, the concept of linguistics readily expands to include graphic and aural communication as well as text-based language. One shared experience of members of the Internet culture is that graphics and text can communicate with equal quality, urgency, and clarity, a concept rarely accepted by readers of print-only materials. The graphic capabilities of the World Wide Web are highly communicative in nature and are in large part a cause of the popular appeal of the Internet and a source of developing intellectual property conflicts. Participants in the Internet culture are like-minded in their acceptance of the graphical element of communication.

In addition, most users who repeatedly use the Internet as a tool for information gathering and communication evaluate and use the materials on the Net on the basis of their inherent qualities. Researchers outside the Internet community often reject sources that are available on the Internet simply because of the appearance of these sources in the networked computer medium. But Internet users learn to distinguish credible sites from those that are not and benefit from access to well-developed materials. In addition, Internet users who regularly participate in on-line communication develop an understanding of the protocols of electronic communication and learn to recognize the markers of a range of on-line personalities. They learn that just as in off-line interaction, social interaction on the Internet creates the possibility of exposure to a wide variety of individuals, including those who are kind, friendly, and helpful, as well as those who are charlatans, criminals, or otherwise dangerous. Members of the Internet community share the concepts that help them to understand these aspects of the on-line culture and maneuver through the system of the Internet. Most members of the Internet community also share a sense of comfort in working with technology that can sometimes be unpredictable in its capability for uploading information or maintaining connections to distant sites, despite their complaints and frustration when systems halt or malfunction. Although they often disagree on how the Internet should progress, what its purposes should be, and how it should be regulated, participants in the Internet community share experiences that allow them to communicate within a common framework of understanding that does not exist for individuals outside the Internet community. They also maintain the common concept that the Internet is a valuable resource and the goal that it should remain viable.

As is true for all social systems, the language of the Internet creates the reality of Net Culture. Even though most individuals who compose the Net community know each other only through the representative electronic texts sent over phone and broad band lines, the special language of the Net creates cohesion: it is the vehicle through which users bind together as members of a socially constructed community. It is through words, and often graphics when in the World Wide Web, that individuals represent themselves. The community of the Internet develops through a connection among digital representations of people who participate on-line. They may be the same participants who make up other off-line communities, but when on-line, they follow constructed, agreed-upon societal mores. "In a community, so it might be said, a man [or woman] is and feels an integral part of an overall way of life, he [or she] is not conscious of a division between his [or her] own attitudes toward the community and the way in which that community organizes and articulates its life. He [or she] is in a full sense a *member* of the community" (Minar and Geer 19) just as in other communities with common goals.

Some of the elements that are common indicators of the manifestation of community are the existence of a group name (Gusfield 34), of a collective experience and a feeling of participation in the creation of the same history (34), and of a mechanism for the maintenance of common traditions (37). Stewart Brand asks, "Want to know where the action in a new culture is? Watch where new language is turning up and where lawyers collect, usually in that sequence" (62). The language of the Internet is well known today. Many people are familiar with terms such as *FAQs, CD ROM,* and *RAM,* and even those who have spent little time on the Internet will know terms such as *netiquette, FTP,* and *download.* Lawyers are certainly collecting to treat Internet-related issues, particularly in intellectual property. Although some may still argue that there can be no culture or community minus a physical locale, broad argument exists that the Internet community requires no physicality and that the cyberspace culture embodies the same markers fit for discussion as those of other communities "on land."[1] Widespread use of Internet technology has made many language markers "old news" to those who have used multiple forms of networked communication in classes, the workplace, and at home, and the broadening acceptance of this "new language" is evidenced by a growing number of allusions to "Internet language" in commercial television and advertising. Nevertheless, there still remain large numbers of people within many segments of society who have never used the current Internet technologies and cannot interpret the language. To share a language that others do not is a prominent marker of community membership.

Legal Multiplicity

Like the community of academicians in humanistic studies and participants on the Internet, the legal community is also constructed and social in nature. The law is not an entity that is easily understood because it is simultaneously a set of rules and regulations, a community, and an academic discipline. However, educators and other individuals interested in affecting the developing intellectual property law must understand what the law is and how it works to become directly involved in the processes that help to create law. In doing so, educators and others who may not accept the ideology that currently drives protectionist applications of law can help to represent nonprotectionist viewpoints. Difficulties in understanding both intellectual property law and the societal impact of our response to the law can be lessened by developing a clear perception of the character and procedural framework of the mechanism of law and of the impact of societal influences on the development of law. The legal community, like others, is socially constructed and driven by the dominant ideological paradigms from which it derives its character. Particularly in law, a socially constructed nature is significant. A good beginning for examining law is to determine its character:

> Law is several things. It is a constantly changing set of norms, or rules and regulations, defining appropriate and prohibited behavior. Law is also a set of prescribed punishments or sanctions for those who violate these norms and a prescription for the way in which these norms are to be enforced and violators punished. (Grossman and Grossman 6)

This characterization of law is the most well known because the regulatory functions of law are most apparent. The legislature intended the regulatory purposes of law to ensure that all citizens can live in safety, to provide forums for settlement of disputes in a peaceful manner, and to allow relative freedom from unfair treatment by those with more physical, political, or economic power. But the law is also intended to support the goals of the Constitution, which enable the rights and freedoms that make up the cultural identity of the United States. It is at this point that characterizing law becomes much more difficult because there is disparity in the interpretations of these freedoms by different individuals and communities.

The law is a set of rules and regulations that govern society in order to preserve order, but it is also the embodiment of a set of principles intended to further societal goals of personal freedom laid out in the Constitution. The law is seemingly static and when most people think of law they think of rules, they either fail to consider or are not aware that the law is a society of people and of ideas, and that the legal society, including all the elements of the community (lawyers, judges, legislators, politicians, and the general public), is socially constructed:

> Law is people. In the United States hundreds of thousands of individuals occupy legal roles or positions, ranging from law enforcement, probation officers and prison guards to prosecutors, private attorneys, judges, legislators, and administrators. To speak of "law" or "legal norms" as a single, definable entity is, of course, an enormous oversimplification. Law is as much a set of formal norms as it is the diverse policies and behavior of these various actors. (6–7)

The processes of negotiation to reach consensus among the disparate groups that affect the legal system are a result of the socially constructed nature of communities. The laws and regulations that dictate our lives were not "found" and brought to society, but were developed within society through negotiative processes that focused on the beliefs and attitudes of differing communities of individuals. It is true that "the law is only a matter of what legal institutions, like legislatures and city councils and courts, have decided in the past" (Dworkin 7), but eventually precedent is revised by adjudicators who interpret past law to fit the needs of the present and, in doing so, create new law that then becomes new precedent. Laws are thus never absolute, but flexible in terms of the influences of communities' ideologies.

To characterize law as socially constructed might at first be unsettling, since society has an interest in maintaining a stable set of laws. A society based on laws and regulations that change without notice or over short durations would be unconstitutional, chaotic, and untenable. Our laws do provide stability because the process of change in legal precedent is slow, soothing the general public by providing an impression that law is foundational in nature. But American law is not based on *absolute* stability. As the national character shifts and circumstances within society change, law must transform and develop to meet those changes. When the law of the past is inadequate to reasonably treat the issues of the present, society then influences a change that can later be overturned by future influences. It is exactly these circumstances that we are facing now as use of the Internet and digitization of information is forcing us to interpret and apply law under new circumstances. Of necessity, the law must be adapted to treat the changing character of information as it morphs into new digital forms.

Judges develop precedential law by deciding legal cases, which is also a socially constructed process. This process actually consists of two mutually supportive goals: To determine the facts of the case at hand and to interpret the law in application to the facts. At first glance, the fact-finding stage of case dispensation seems to be relatively absent of societal influence. Participants in the fact-finding process testify to what they saw, did, or heard regarding relevant parties to the case. However, participants do not give testimony purely in isolation, but from community influenced perceptions. Witness testimony is based on culturally determined bases of understanding. For instance, educators may fear legal statutes and want to know the exact boundaries within which they can use copyrighted materials, particularly when they begin to teach in distance learning forums. They may want to know whether they can use a digital copy of an article in an on-line classroom. But lawyers know that the boundaries of the law may change from case to case and that some courts broaden the boundaries, whereas others narrow them. A court whose ideology mirrors that of a foundationalist community would be more likely to find the use of the digital copy and infringement, whereas a court that follows a constructionist ideology, supportive of public access, would be less so. The law is not only a series of rules and regulations but is a social construct, tied to the values of the communities in which it is applied.

The legislative process is also dialogic and depends on negotiation among conflicting members of communities with differing points of view who have to arrive at a final legal outcome. It is a process of negotiation in which congresspeople, elected on the basis of constituent support of their own goals and purposes, work toward making their objectives (and thus the objectives of their constituents) accepted as common goals of the nation. This process requires argument, and dissensus arises while various representatives of different communities of constituents pursue goals at cross-purposes. But law is eventually made or revised as a result of this process of argument, negotiation, and final resolution of conflict through the sheer force of power behind a majority of congressional votes. Seemingly, the issues supported by the dissenting minority are defeated and disappear from any further aspect of legislation. But paradigms shift as dissensus is interjected into the negotiative conversation (Kuhn, Feyerabend). In law, the continual influence of new opinion, in the form of congressional argument repeated over time, eventually wears down the opposition until a new consensus of thought is reached and new law is made. The dialogic nature of the legislative process also allows room for influence from sources outside legal bodies. Educators and individual citizens, with a clear understanding of the law applied in diligent pursuit of support of public access, can affect the way the intellectual property law is interpreted and influence legislators to note the positive effect of public access to information and the negative effect of its lack.

The legislative process notwithstanding, extralegislative actions of separate communities within society also have an impact on what the law is and what the rules and regulations of law become. Communities within society influence the character of the national culture, our national personality, in such a way that our laws and their ultimate ends embody what we are as a society. The written law is not a powerful entity in itself, but is only as powerful as the force of the community of individuals who legitimize it:

> [T]he true grounds of law lie in the acceptance by the community as a whole of a fundamental master rule . . . that assigns to a particular people or groups the authority to make law. So propositions of law are true not just in virtue of the commands of people who are habitually obeyed, but more fundamentally in virtue of social conventions that represent the community's acceptance of a scheme of rules empowering such people to create valid law. (Hart in Dworkin 34)

Even positivist interpretations of law that mandate specific action based on accepted precedential law must be tempered by adjudicators' interpretations of that law.[2] As rigid as the field of law may seem on the surface, in actuality, and by necessity, it is an area rife with flexibility: "Modern societies share a belief in the directive power of government and law. None believes absolutely in the fixity and permanence of law" (Friedman 38). In fact, the concept of flexibility is purposely built into the law to allow for interpretation. This idea may seem discomforting, but flexibility is necessary for making law work in a nation of many subcultures, racial and national influences, opinions, mores, and standards.

Sandford Levinson and J. M. Balkin illustrate the concept of statutory interpretation through a treatise on the musical interpretation of Beethoven's music. Beethoven wrote in the first movement of his first piano concerto a piece that calls for a high F-natural where an F-sharp is really needed. Many conductors interpret his choice as one made because at that time the piano had no F-sharp even though the piece called for it. They believe that Beethoven thought ahead to the capacity of the piano of the future, but wrote the F-natural to acquiesce to the limits of the day. Modern-day conductors are left to interpret the piece and decide whether to play an F-sharp or F-natural in their performances

(58). The conundrum of a conductor's choices in playing Beethoven is similar to that of adjudicators who must interpret law. If a law is written too narrowly, the implied intent for future use would be lost and there would be no room to interpret the law to fit the needs of the particular society upon which it is enforced or to fit the needs of the particular time in which it is to be applied. Law is situational. If the law were written too loosely, the potential lawbreaker would have no fair understanding of the requirements of law and the due process mandated by the Constitution would not be met. The judge or jury, as well, would have no guidelines with which to dispense with conflict and carry out the regulation of society; therefore, the law would fail to meet its purpose. The law must then be flexible, but not too flexible, in order to enable its adjustment to an ever-changing society.

Controlling Political Access

Our unique system of government requires participation from all its citizens for creating laws by which all must abide. In essence, members of society are not bound by law through force but through mutual agreement; however, because participation in government operates through a process of representation, many individuals lose sight of the participatory character of government. It becomes tacit rather than explicit. Nevertheless, history illustrates that American citizens will abide only by law that they find acceptable, and the creation of that acceptability requires that communities acknowledge diverse thought in the law's development. "[D]emocracy implies continuous interaction between formal institutions and ever-evolving practices of popular participation. Democracy also means struggle and disagreement over the very meaning of the word" (Andrews and Chapman 5). The processes involved in participatory democracy parallel the social construction of communities through negotiation toward reaching consensus:

> [Hart] said that the true grounds of law lie in the acceptance by the community as a whole of a fundamental master rule (he called this a "rule of recognition") that assigns to a particular people or groups the authority to make law. So propositions of law are true not just in virtue of the commands of people who are habitually obeyed, but more fundamentally in virtue of social conventions that represent the community's acceptance of a scheme of rules empowering such people to create valid law. (Dworkin 34)

The process of negotiation must also be flexible, allowing the introduction of disparate views so that growth and adaptation of law can occur:

> While system and integration are essential, flexibility and constant revision are no less so. Law is the dynamic process in which few

> solutions can be permanent. Hence, . . . the redefinition of relations
> and the reorientation of expectancies. Initiative and scope of work
> means new problems for the law. New inventions, new ideas, new
> behaviors keep creeping in. . . . Then the law is called in to decide
> what principles shall be applied to conflicts of claims rooted in dis-
> parate cultures. Do the new claims fit comfortably to the old pos-
> tulates? Must the newly realized ways of behaving be wholly rejected
> and legally suppressed because they are out of harmony with the old
> values? (Hoebel 275–81)

Often, the concept of negotiating for consensus tends to overempha-
size the need for like-mindedness in a way that implies that there is value
in maintaining a nation submerged in "groupthink." In actuality, dissensus is necessary to a healthy process of establishing law. "Law in the
United States is a multiplicity of people and processes frequently operating at cross-purposes rather than in concert" (Grossman and Grossman 6–7). The concept of participatory democracy (through which federal law is created and state law is influenced) is based on the expectation
that differing political forces will hammer out their differences through
a national dialogic process. "Democracy requires a host of cultural practices—habits of mind, rituals of participation, forms of dialogue between
ruler and ruled—that make large numbers of people across generations
believe in the meaningfulness of basic democratic principles" (Andrews
and Chapman 6). Dissensus is not only expected but valuable; the result of conflictual collaboration is the inception of more creative ideas
and more effective solutions to problems (Weiss in Lay and Karis 46).
By its very nature, the process of negotiating toward consensus requires
that the better-supported argument wins out over that which is weak.
Social ideologists argue that the dialogic process is actually nonegali-
tarian because it enables the more politically powerful to assimilate those
with weaker support into the dominant paradigm of thought (Berlin,
Myers, and Miller in Blyler and Thralls 15). At a minimum, however, a
dialogic process allows for contributions from weaker factions that, if
persuasive, have the potential to become the new paradigm:

> This pattern of agreement and disagreement is temporary. . . . Sud-
> denly what seemed unchallengeable is challenged, a new or even
> radical interpretation of some important part of legal practice is
> developed in someone's chambers or study which then finds favor
> within a "progressive" minority. Paradigms are broken, and new
> paradigms emerge. (Dworkin 89–90)

Dissensus does affect change in law and government, notwithstanding
its gradual nature. But in order to allow for dissensus, minority voices
must be heard. Accommodating dissensus ensures that a diversity of
American opinions can be acknowledged, if not through direct recep-

tion into the political process, then through other means of acknowledgment in government development.

The average citizen's predominant avenue for participation in government is through representation by elected officials. Although the difficulty in becoming apprised of complicated legal and political issues and the extensiveness of the population makes representative government necessary, this system tends to separate citizens from the real action of the dialogic process. Many individuals feel isolated from real lawmaking processes and feel underrepresented. The tendency is to view government as an opposing force instead of a force of which all citizens are a part. Most often, "legal argument takes place on a plateau of rough consensus that if law exists it provides a justification for the use of collective power against individual citizens or groups" (108–9). Individuals, as a consequence, feel separated from the political process. Individuals with conflicting voices must have access to the dialogic political process, both for becoming educated about the content of contrary opinions and for voicing dissenting, minority opinion.

Societal law, developed through community custom, is created outside the organized processes of litigation and legislation. Law developed through custom can, nonetheless, have an important impact on developing new case and statutory law and on applying existing law. It is, therefore, important to note its existence. There is a distinction between "made law" (statutory law) and "implied law" (custom) (Fuller 70–71) but neither is pure; implicit law always resides in statutes and "conscious creation enters into the rules of customary law" (70). The rules of customary law "find their implicit expression in the conduct itself" (71), and their purpose is never explicitly expressed. Statutory law, on the other hand, gains its power from the explicit expression of its purpose.

The concept that "law is a matter of historical decisions by people in positions of political power has never wholly lost its grip on jurisprudence" (Dworkin 34), but the law is actually much more flexible than it seems on its surface. Although those with political and economic power often strongly influence the interpretation and development of law, it is more difficult to notice that through both action and inaction as collective communities, groups in society have the power to shape not only the laws themselves but their enforcement.

We know that when individuals, groups, or corporations break laws they are subject to sanction of one kind or another and that the sanction they receive is often dictated by their relational power in society. What we often fail to see (or disregard as irrelevant because of its seeming lack of influence) is the power of community action and inaction to affect changes in law. Relatively few laws are changed through the legislative political process, and those that are change very slowly. But a powerful means of influence that is often ignored is the treatment of laws by citizens and the power we have to create change by the sheer force of the development and redevelopment of societal mores that affect interpretation of law: "No law printed on paper ever came to life without some cultural input; in which case, it is the culture which is the sole source of effectiveness for law" (Friedman 33). Indicative of the kind of power that communities have to affect change, the existence of "blue laws," common to every state, demonstrates that law can be "changed" through processes outside legislative procedures. Blue laws are those laws that have never been repealed yet are never enforced. The influence of community standards have in effect made laws obsolete, thus, "blue." These laws stay on the books despite their obsolescence because the economic and temporal cost of the legislative procedure to remove them would be prohibitive. In effect, the participants in society, in both the legal and extralegal communities, have negotiated an agreement to ignore the existence of these laws. But a law that is "blue" may also, through societal renegotiation, be reconstituted. In the 1960s, television script writing was limited by FCC regulations that censored content and expressive terms that were considered "off color." In the 1990s, however, although the network censors continue to impose limits on television scripts, the standards are much more lax, at least in part because community views have changed: "The legislatures may be formally charged with setting legal norms. But the willingness of the courts, the police and others to enforce these norms is the crucial determinant of what sort of impact a particular legal norm will have" (Grossman and Grossman 7).

Where citizens have been underrepresented in political arenas, it has become more common to create a voice through access to the legal, rather than the political, system. For instance, the tobacco lobby has been so strong in Washington, D.C., that the Federal Drug Administration (FDA) has been slow to inhibit tobacco companies' production and sale of harmful tobacco products. In attempts to curtail the development and sale of tobacco products, groups of affected parties have banded together in filing class action suits against tobacco companies to recover for damages. Although these suits have not stopped tobacco production, they have focused attention on tobacco companies' responsibilities to the public and have created a climate in which these companies have come under closer scrutiny by consumer groups and the FDA. Influenced by the strength of public opinion, the legislature has begun consideration of these issues as well. In this case, participatory government has developed by way of societal influence in the legal system rather than through political channels. Mikhail Bakhtin and Jürgen Habermas's discussions of "the dialogic" and "communicative action" are helpful for understanding how an egalitarian democratic process operates.

Political Access: Communicative Action and the Dialogic

Mikhail Bakhtin and Jürgen Habermas describe a dialogic process and a framework of communicative action, showing how constructed communities can advance participatory government by supporting political access for all community participants. These philosophers' works substantiate the importance of community participation for influencing the political frameworks of societies and illustrate why broad participation from members of academic, legal, and Internet communities is important for creating societal structures that reflect the ideologies of diverse communities. Particularly at a time where the introduction and use of the Internet is moving legislators and other legal professionals to reconsider interpretations and application of intellectual property law, educators, individuals, and others who can play a role in affecting the developing law should note the operation of communicative action and the dialogic process. For Bakhtin, every form of communication consists of a multiplicity of voices and meanings that all contain a dialogic, an exchange of ideas and opinions. The individual is not lost within the confines of a community but is able to provide an individual voice that contributes to constructing the shared reality of that community. In Bakhtin's view, "the dialogic process is concerned with creating alternatives or even antithetical semantic and ideological positions which are defined by the dialectical interplay among the constitutive voices" (Thibault 111). His "concept of the multiaccented 'word' . . . implies multiple, even contradictory value orientations which are implicit in the 'word'" (111). The means of exploring the relative positions of people in the community is language. For Kenneth Bruffee, the community is shaped by the discourse it produces (774) and for Bakhtin, "[l]anguage is taken to be the expression of an already given social reality. Dialogic discourse restores to textual practice the material interplay of frequently opposing and contradictory semantic and ideological positions which actively constitute the formation of discourse" (Thibault 90). The exchange of ideas that not only describes but creates societal structures is inherently dialogic, even in authoritarian societies. Even those voices that are censored or ignored are a part of what Bakhtin coins "heteroglossia." "Here Bakhtin's idea that language is always multiple is crucial. Language, in other words, is always borrowed, shared, and alien as well as mine" (Shevstova 753). Where collaboration to develop consensus is "the conversation of mankind" (Oakeshott qtd. in Bruffee 638), just as conversation derives consensus from dissensus, Bakhtin's view of the dialogic process points to no less than a negotiation process in which the basis of consensus changes with the development and acceptance of new knowledge. "The dialogic process ensures that differences and conflicts in a state of continual dialectical interplay actually constitute the structure. Structural change occurs when these conflicts bring about a resolution or readjustment on some other level in the system" (Thibault 113), and "the dialogic mode offers the possibility for change and a developing point of view" (Danow 120) in which the very existence of a contradictory voice contributes to social change. Following Bakhtin's reasoning, it is not only possible but important to include representative voices from communities whose ideologies do not support the legal status quo when interpreting and redeveloping intellectual property law. Ironically, the very Internet technology that has incited so much recent protectionist-oriented legislative and adjudicative activity is also a forum for the dialogic that Bakhtin describes.

Although *heteroglossia* is the embodiment of a chaotic cacophony of multiple voices, each in turn resounding against one another, the atmosphere that it creates is not counterproductive but, rather, inclusive. "Resistance conceived of as a form of life consists of dissensus without conflict, a momentarily detotalizing opposition to the value system of rationalization in favor of the value of life, and a *jouissance* that accounts for the sociality of resistance and its capacity to endure" (Halley 168). This metacommunicative situation "represents the co-existence of socio-ideological contradictions between the present and past . . . between different socio-ideological groups in the present, between tendencies, schools, circles, and so forth, all given a bodily form" (San Juan Jr. 76).

Lawrence and Timberg, and Berlin, Myers, Miller, and Bizzell, academic humanists who subscribe to an ideologic social constructionist approach, emphasize the political power of social construction (Blyler and Thralls 6): that is, the process ensures that participants are assimilated into a community where those with more hierarchical power determine the accepted basis of belief to which all others must subscribe. Even those who emphasize the effect of relational power within the process of social construction, however, cannot deny the influence of the dialogic. But according to Bakhtin's view of the dialogic process, the existence of a chaotic conglomeration of multiple views allows for change in an inhumane and antagonistic power structure that can negate the voices of its marginalized citizens. Bakhtin supports the existence of heteroglossia as "the equality-inducing destratifying signs of authentic sociality found in the carnivalesque moments of popular life" (Halley 167). Supporting a dialogic process of construction of shared reality acknowledges the contradicting segments in society and becomes the first step toward antihegemonic change.

Jürgen Habermas also poses a form of dialogism that he calls communicative action as a means of empowering marginalized segments of society: acknowledgment of social construction as an organizational framework of communities is also an acknowledgment of the power of communication in society and the need to provide access to communication from all levels of society. As a basis for communicative action, Habermas has broadened the application of Max Weber's use of the term *rationalization* to mean "the extension of the areas of society subject to the criteria of rational decision" and the industrialization of social labor, "with the result that criteria of instrumental action also penetrate into other areas of life" (Habermas, *Toward a Rational Society* 81). More important for its application, however, is Habermas's further explanation that, "what Weber called 'rationalization' realizes not rationality as such, but rather, in the name of rationality, a specific form of unacknowledged political domination" (82). Acknowledgment that communities are socially constructed is tantamount to acknowledging the need to give voice to the voiceless in order to provide resistance to rationalization:

> [T]he confrontation between a rationalizing tendency and a desire to assert the conditions of choice. . . . These conditions of choice are tied, not to consensus, but to difference in the form of dissensus without conflict . . . a difference tolerated and even encouraged. . . . This is what is carnivalesque, and radically democratic, in cultural and popular mobilizations. . . . (Halley 166)

Although Habermas is not generally considered a social constructionist who disregards the existence of a philosophical foundation, he declares that there is no need for foundational knowledge: "Pragmatism and hermeneutics, in replacing an epistemological stance, 'accord a higher position to acting and speaking than to knowing'" (*Theory of Communicative Action* 304). He supports the concept that individual access to communication through social interaction constructs the society in which its players exist:

> Under the functional aspect of coordinating action, [communicative action] serves social integration and the establishment of solidarity; . . . under the aspect of socialization, communicative action serves the formation of personal identities. The symbolic structures of the lifeworld are reproduced by way of the continuation of valid knowledge, stabilization of group solidarity, and socialization of responsible actors. (331)

Habermas argues that language is a constituted collective practice that binds its users together in the life-world (Olafsen 656) in which "[d]iscourse is the medium within which individual reason and collective reason will converge" (Warren 213); thus, he supports the concept that through language, the reality of a culture is created.

Works by philosophers such as Bakhtin and Habermas provide a basis, not only for understanding the effect of socially constructed thought on community, but as Habermas makes clear in particular, understanding how participation in the dialogic, the conversation of the culture, is necessary for political representation of society's participants. In order to develop intellectual property law in response to the new issues that arise as a result of the Internet and digitization of information, the legislative and adjudicative processes that create law should account for the needs of all represented ideologies in our society of widely dissimilar interests and cultures. Joining the uncontrolled voices of all society's participants is necessary for inclusive national dialogue. Although reaching consensus about what the law should be is not without conflict, it is the dissonance that is necessary for representing a spectrum of ideological beliefs within legal structures.

Dissonance, Conflict, and Negotiating Power

A positivist defines the process of assimilation into a community as the acceptance of one static foundational "Truth" that, supported by authority, is dictated to all members of a community. In contrast, one who believes in social construction supports acceptance of change brought on by dissonance created through a dialogic process by which each individual in a community contributes to the construction of the community itself.

If reality is socially constructed, different communities in society construct differing realities (Berger and Luckman 1). The synthesis of ideas from individuals of disparate backgrounds is what makes these communities special because they negotiate from their unique perspectives toward a consensus that represents members of the community. However, this is not to say that once individuals come together to support the construction of a community with like goals and ideals, the bases of belief will never change. Ideologic foundations of "truth" can be changed by outside influences, and constructions of "truth" always depend on social conditions (16). Although community interaction has a regulatory effect and limits what is admitted into a community's body of knowledge (Blyler and Thralls 7–10), new influences such as the fresh ideas from individuals new to the community will continue to affect constructed groups. When new participants introduce different ideas they, in turn, affect the dominant beliefs and create dissensus from which growth and change occurs. Even in a society that is grounded in a belief in positivism, like the scientific community, paradigms of thought are changed by the influences of new ideas (Kuhn). Conceptual anarchy can influence the way that established and powerful scientific entities change their conception of "fact" (Feyerabend). Communities are not limited in developing and revising what is considered knowledge; they create knowledge through consensual agreement instead (Blyler and Thralls 17–18).

Communities of academicians in humanistic studies, professionals in the legal community, and participants on the Internet are subject to the same kinds of changes that all constructed societies experience. Each of these communities is characterized by its own set of conventions of language and discourse (Bruffee 11), and nonmembers must go through a process of internalization of community norms before acquiring membership (12). Literate communities such as these are created and recreated through their writing. "[W]e make social reality, including social structure, over and over again in the interactions and interpretations in which we are engaged" (Brandt 34) because literacy itself is social and a social construct: in literate communities the *conversation* among community members in the form of journal publications, legal briefs, newsletters, e-mail, websites, and books becomes a functional framework of thought that represents the dominant paradigms of the community.

Howard Rheingold makes the point that cyberspace is the place for a rebirth of community (26), which is made possible by technology that allows like-minded individuals to bind together virtually by way of a meshing of ideas. The virtual space of the Net is a "third place" (25–26, 171, 224), with no less potential to unite individuals than the local coffee shop or the neighborhood recreation center. Legal, academic humanist, and Internet communities clash, as well as merge, at their meeting points in cyberspace.

To develop community no longer requires physical presence or homogeneity (Gusfield 32). In fact, it was never physical presence that created community before the development and use of networked technology but the sharing of ideas to struggle toward a consensus in what the Internet should be. Douglass Rushkoff describes a reversal of communal roles of physical presence and the Internet in his chronicles of the development of a face-to-face community in San Francisco that arose from on-line relationships. As he describes it, this is a community that intersperses on-line and off-line relationships in such a way that individuals make no distinction between the two.

The Internet functions to link individuals through ideas, and it is this very practice that makes it a powerful creator of socially constructed communities. These community members are bound together even through their conflicting conversations with one another. Rather than like-mindedness, negotiation through communal conflict is required for further development of the culture. Computer-mediated communication encourages engaged participation in written discourse. Electronic discourse allows more egalitarian access to community discussion, thus more interaction among community members. It is in the ether of the interaction and the interconnectedness itself that the community is made. The epistemology of social construction points to the importance of the social dimension of knowledge, and the Internet provides a forum for polyvalent discourse by which all participants in the culture can be heard, encouraging greater participation among all community members in the dialogic process. The Internet culture is the embodiment of the heteroglossia that makes up a socially constructed community and gives political voice to all participants.

People have been searching for such a sense of belonging for some time now. The "Beat Generation" of the 1950s, once more developing popularity for its mimicry of the isolation and lack of community exemplified in J. D. Salinger's *Catcher in the Rye,* is indicative of the feeling of alienation of many individuals in a society always increasing in complexity and isolation. "Surely the outstanding characteristic of contemporary thought on man [or woman] and society is the preoccupation with personal alienation and cultural disintegration" (Nisbet 3). The individual as a person connected to the workplace, home, *and* political society has become a thing of the past: "The modern world . . . with its progressive division of labour and the development of mass urban society had destroyed the idea of the whole man. In modern society man was now a narrow and enervated being and the nature of his [/her] social contacts had become more and more fragmented" (Minar and Geer 17). Society has become so heavily bureaucratized that individuals feel out of touch with their places within it:

> A further major feature in man[/woman]'s contemporary condition which preoccupied those who formed the sociological tradition of which our present understanding of community is a part, and which indeed has continued to influence contemporary thinking on community, has been the increasing organisation and bureacratisation of life generally but in particular in the sphere of politics. . . . [W]ith the development of the industrial revolution, political, economic and social power has become increasingly centralised and in consequence men[/women] have come to feel less and less at home in the social world; they have become estranged from that social world in which they live, move and have their being. (19)

Individuals have felt a general sense of uselessness and a lack of effectiveness in the political processes since the hippie movements of the 1960s (Toffler). The sense of separation from society and its political processes is growing:

> The individual citizen has ceased to have any sense of his[/her] be-
> ing personally involved: he[/she] no longer feels that he[/she] is able
> to identify him[/her]self with any organised body. . . . The main
> question then is how to promote greater flexibility in institutions and
> to increase their systematic contact with the population or, to put it
> differently how to transform formal democracy so that it becomes
> a living democracy. Conscious participation of the population in the
> development of their own community and readiness to share respon-
> sibility are essential if that transformation is to take place. (Hendricks
> qtd. in Minar and Geer 59)

The Internet provides a forum where culture can draw participants into
a community in which individuals can feel that they have at least some
power to create a community that reflects their own desires and goals.
While everything else in society seems increasingly bureaucratized, participants in the Internet community are finding it a great "wide open
space" in which they are free to build a community from scratch, a community with a true participatory democracy in which they have a real,
tangible impact on what the community becomes. Note the impact of
Internet reports by Matt Drudge, an uncredentialed, unknown Internet
reporter, in initiating news reports of President Clinton's affair with a
White House intern (Drudge Report).

By its very nature, the connectivity of the Internet mandates that what
the community will become, what the Internet community *is,* is determined through a negotiation of reality created by the participation of
all individuals who log on-line. It is important to remember that a community is not a *ding an sich* that lives a life of its own and exists in the
absence of people. The community is an abstract concept that denotes
the interconnection of individuals:

> A social relationship will be called "communal" (Vergemein-
> schaftung) if and so far as the orientation of social action—whether
> in the individual case, on the average, or in the pure type, is based
> on a subjective feeling of the parties, whether affectual or traditional,
> that they belong together. A social relationship will be called "asso-
> ciative" (Vergesellschaftung) if and in so far as the orientation of
> social action within it rests on a rationally motivated adjustment of
> interests or a similarly motivated agreement, whether the basis of
> rational judgment be absolute values or reasons of expediency.
> (Gusfield 11)

It is only natural that a sense of community would grow from participants on the Internet. The Internet gives users the power to speak and
be heard, and when participation in a community can mean that "the
individual sees him[/her]self as able to exercise some degree of volun-
tary control over his[/her] behavior" (Glen 17), a feeling of membership

is the next result. Although most of us easily learn to master the process of assimilating into communities, "[w]e learn too that society will expect a certain degree of conformity to its norms and that there are penalties for failure as well as rewards for success" (21). But despite pressures to conform to the community in the form of fear of exclusion for being different and the reward of security and support that follow acceptance (20), membership in the Internet community does not proscribe individual opinion; in fact, it does quite the contrary. Usenet News, for example, provides a connection point for more than ten thousand electronic bulletin boards, containing a full range of discussion topics from all areas of popular culture, politics, sports, drama, music, art, family, religion, and others. The incredible diversity of a worldwide range of participants who post and receive e-mail on a daily basis is a good indication of individual thought, yet all these participants, in all their diversity, still maintain a constructed community. "Conflict with others and the resulting cooperation and common struggle often provide the experiences from which an aggregate of people develop a sense of themselves as possessed of a common fate and belonging to a common group" (Gusfield 36). Just as face-to-face involvement and common physical territory are not required for membership in a community, neither is homogeneity (32).

The Internet culture is made up of individuals with a broad range of differing opinions and ideas, but these individuals are united by a common desire for linguistic (both textual and graphical) communication that creates connections among them and, in turn, creates community. The Internet is a metaphorical map of a constructed society in which individuals share information and graphic expressions, use each others' texts as a basis for comment and criticism, and encourage collaborative thinking processes. It is the embodiment of the constructionist ideology. But the Internet has also become a flash point for conflict between constructionist and foundational ideologies where creators fear misuse or appropriation of their creative expressions, made easy by the function of Internet technology. Examining the dominant ideologies of the legal, Internet, and academic humanist communities and noting how each would interpret and apply intellectual property law reveal conflicts that must be treated in intellectual property law's development in response to the Internet.

6

Controlling Ideologies: The Internet, Law, and Humanistic Studies

Ideology drives a community's valuation of societal goals, its understanding of "property" by way of definition of authorship and ownership, and its interpretations of the goals of the intellectual property statute. Examining the differences among representative ideologies of the Internet, legal, and academic humanist communities reveals a basis for conflict that is significant for understanding differing interpretations of the existing intellectual property statute and the potential influence on the developing intellectual property law.

The mutual interests of the academic, professional, and social communities of academic humanists, law professionals, and Internet participants sometimes conflict when they interpret the concept of "property" in intellectual property law. In addition, the differing ideologies of these three communities influence interpretations of property and form the basis for administering the law that affects how intellectual creations are produced and treated. Furthermore, each community's ideologies influence one another and are affected by concepts of ownership, authorship, and authority, which all derive from concepts of property. These multiple influences, in turn, provide a basis for influencing intellectual property law further and creating an impact on production and use of print and digital works in the future. Each community's view of how knowledge is created is significant for influencing the intellectual property law that was promulgated to support its creative process.

James Berlin locates three predominant ideologies of belief in how knowledge is created: objective (foundational, positivist), subjective (expressivist, Romantic), and transactional (social constructionist) (6). The objective epistemology calls for concrete evidence and does not allow for private vision or social arrangements. It is based in positivism, requires current traditional teaching (7), and allows instructors to claim superior power and privilege (78). The objectivist epistemology, based upon scientific method, allows its proponents to contend that knowledge is discovered through application of tests that will help to locate absolute objective answers. The subjective or expressivist view locates truth in the individual (11) if the Romantic concept of knowledge creation is followed. Followers of this epistemology isolate themselves in the acts of creating knowledge, assuming that original work derives from individual effort. The transactional epistemology explains that truth arises from interaction between subject and object, subject and audience, or language and social construction (15) and acknowledges that new knowledge is created through interaction among members of a community.

The dominant epistemological choice of a community has a significant impact on how that view will play out in a consideration of property and ownership. Both positivist and expressivist viewpoints are based on a concept of ownership that focuses on isolated nonchanging views of knowledge. Positivists locate knowledge through experimentation, then claim ownership in the discovery, and expressivists claim that knowledge is produced by the individual in isolation from other influences and claim ownership in the creation of individual original work. Both of these viewpoints negate the possibility of influence from outside sources for collaborative knowledge creation and disavow the characterization of one document as jointly owned unless it was obviously coauthored; they both acknowledge exclusive control of unchanging wisdom.

In contrast, proponents of the transactional view, based on the epistemology of social construction, believe that knowledge is never created in isolation but is affected by outside influences of the community. Despite the overwhelming adherence to belief in positivism in the field of science, even scientific "facts" are socially constructed and change as dissonant community influences affect the dominant paradigm by introducing new competing paradigms (Kuhn, Feyerabend). Moreover, a belief in social construction supports the view that ownership in knowledge is shared and denies exclusive claim to its development or use. Social construction emphasizes community over the individual and places proprietorship of knowledge in the hands of society at large. A social constructionist view is consistent with the views of users' rights proponents who support the constitutional purpose of ensuring access to information. This ideology supports the often-ignored policy goals of the constitutional intellectual property provision, that information must be available to the public in order to build new knowledge while also participating in the dialogic process of influencing culture. The dominant ideological perspectives of educators in humanistic studies and participants in the Internet community favor a view of property, ownership, and authority that is nonexclusive, nonauthoritarian, and egalitarian. The technology of the digital world and the beliefs of the community that are growing from it are influencing society's views toward defining authorship, ownership, and property, and are continuing to deepen its influence on the academic humanist community's commitment to the same ideals.

Digitizing "Property"

The impact of technology on intellectual property has continued to be a force, even as technology advances. Constructionist ideologies support a belief that communities create knowledge collaboratively, and the digitization of information and Internet communication provide metaphorical illustrations of this belief. Foundational, Romantic views of knowledge creation, however, clash with concepts that communities create knowledge through a process of negotiation. The invention and use of the Gutenberg press created a collective ideological change in how property was defined, replacing the narrow view of property as an entity that could remain under the physical control of only one owner with a concept of property as an entity that could be simultaneously owned and sold. The Internet takes this ideological change light-years forward in its capability to transfer digitized information in a matter of seconds, uninhibited by distances of global proportions.

Nicholas Negroponte, director of the Massachusetts Institute of Technology's Media Lab, claims that there has been a change in world exchange from atoms to bits (3–4). Atoms, he explains, make up physical entities such as books and ledgers, where bits are the sole components of digitized materials. Information that is contained in the form of atoms has substance and is weighty, difficult to transport, and difficult to modify. Digital information, on the other hand, is ephemeral and weightless, transports in seconds, and can be modified quickly and substantially. Like the character of hypertext, "[b]eing digital . . . creates the potential for new content to originate from a whole new combination of sources" (Negroponte 19). In the days of atoms, merely having possession of a book, sheet of music, or booklet of poetry meant that the owner had possession of the ideas, furthering the Romantic concept of authorship, which in effect supported the concept that the author owned the ideas. The difficulty in accessing information was in the limited ability to buy the actual physical form of the book, hampered by high cost or unavailability. The mere use of digitized materials changes the focus of ownership from the physical object of the container to the information that is held within it. Where the physical limitations of a book allow for breadth *or* depth, bits in the form of digitized expressions allow for both breadth *and* depth in the same volume (68–69) and an efficient means to transport information. Without a field of containment for information, differing kinds of media can easily commingle to the degree that it is inevitable that almost every digital work will be developed from contributions of multiple creators who play roles as writers, musicians, artists, and even technical advisers. According to Negroponte, "[i]nteraction is implicit in all multimedia" (70).

Even primitive word-processor technology changes a user's thinking patterns and abilities by providing the writer with the capability to think spontaneously (Heim 152) in a way that combines private thought and public text (193) and creates a more social dimension of writing (163). Constructed language, a socially influenced phenomenon, becomes thinking and moves language into the realm of information exchange:

> Treated as information, language becomes a transparent vehicle for what is already determined existentially. That is to say "in-formation" is already formed by the network of involvements in which it is exchanged; information takes place in a world that is presumed to already have been formed. (Heim 86–87)

If the relatively simple technology of the word processor can change the way people think, the impact of digitized text on social organization is even farther reaching. Shoshana Zuboff conducted an extensive study of the introduction of technology into the workplace and found that technology eliminates the need for a physical culture but requires instead an "intellective culture" in which people have to go through a different thinking process than they do with nontechnologized culture (196). For instance, she points out that in a technology-based work environment, a manager's job might be to program machines to conduct self-repair rather than physically repair the mechanical problem itself. The ability to analyze a problem and (through a synthesis of consideration of a number of options) apply the necessary information is essential in a technological environment. To resolve problems in a technological age, a worker must have the ability to access information, then synthesize it to create effective solutions to problems. In the past, a manager's power depended on exclusive control of the knowledge base (6). In a technological society, the required knowledge base is too broad to be contained in one individual or corporation; the cognitive contributions of many participants are required. In addition, each individual must maintain social networks with others in order to access the information he or she needs. The means for surviving in the workplace has as much to do with the ability to assimilate into appropriate communities as to manage a corporate bankroll. The Internet makes use of computers to amplify human thinking and communication (Rheingold 66), which "has to do with the way groups of people are using computer-mediated communication to rediscover the power of cooperation, turning cooperation into a game, a way of life—a merger of knowledge capital, social capital, and communion" (110). The relatively new means of developing and using knowledge in the Internet community evidences the impact of technology on forming an ideological paradigm:

> The current trigger for a transition into a new stage, in Kumon's theory, is the world telecommunications network, and the next game will involve information, knowledge, and folklore-sharing cooperatives around the world that will challenge the primacy of traditional wealth the way industrial wealth challenged the primacy of military and national power and prestige. (210)

Today's virtual communities are a model of societies that work from collective wealth (210).

The Internet community's ideological position regarding property, authorship, and authority has an immense impact on the way we view intellectual creation:

> These last years of the century seem full of flux and controversy particularly at that interface of culture and technology we call writing. Issues of interpretation, authority, literacy, and textuality gain salience in a society driven by transaction in information. The idea into itself seems to be shifting, becoming less a matter of content than of association, less monolithic truth than polyvalent discourse. (Moulthrop and Kaplan 220)

Members of the Internet community have come to expect that language is a social construct and that the information contained in it is collectively created. Despite the influx of numerous commercial entities on the Internet, the dominant ideological stance of the community of the Internet (evidenced through action) is one that values cooperation, collaboration, and the sharing of ideas to support the furtherance of knowledge above all else. Even the CNI-IP e-mail discussion list, populated primarily by lawyers and law professors who practice, teach, or otherwise have an interest in intellectual property issues bears out that sharing information is an accepted goal on the Internet; members of the list often entertain requests for information and sources and respond readily when asked. They also quote other message posters' texts freely and frequently.

Some academic organizations with particular interests in digitized information and Internet participation are beginning to mirror the collaborative activities for knowledge building that occur on the Internet.

Nicholas Negroponte established the Media Lab at MIT as an electronic think tank and production arena in which MIT students, some of the leading computer programming and electronic engineering students in the country, develop new insights into technology, then produce their ideas. Through an unusual move for an academic director, Negroponte, founder of the Media Lab, solicited funding for his experimental lab from wealthy corporate donors but funded it in a nonproprietary way to help each contributor to the project gain access to more of the information developed. Although, at first, corporate contributors found the concept of sharing information contrary to their paradigm of exclusive ownership, they have found that this arrangement better suits their needs because they have access to more information for less money (Brand 156–57).

Someday all the information that exists in the world will be on the Internet, and that the container of the ideas will no longer be necessary:

> Once that has happened, all the goods of the Information Age—all of the expressions once contained in books or film strips or news-letters—will exist either as pure thought or something very much like pure thought; voltage conditions darting around the Net at the speed of light, in conditions that one might behold in effect, as glowing pixels or transmitted sounds, but never touch or claim to "own" in the old sense of the word. (Barlow)

The consensus of thought among those who analyze participants in the Internet community is that sharing of information is good for the individual, as well as for society. Ownership in shared information by the public at large encourages new knowledge and is economically advantageous to all participants. Once a communal conversation occurs on the Internet, the community can claim ownership because the community as a whole takes part in its creation. This relatively new means of connection among individuals and separate, distinct communities introduces a new era of thought about ownership and authority where "[a]ll questions about community in Cyberspace point to a similar kind of transition that might be taking place now, for which we have no technical names" (Rheingold 64). The ideology that drives the Internet community is one that supports collaborative creation and knowledge sharing where no one participant claims exclusive ownership.

Digitization of text and Internet communication have incited new thought and discussion regarding the character of intellectual creations, their authorship, and ownership. Academicians in humanistic studies and Internet participants most often find the discussion supportive of their communities' ideological goals, whereas most members of the legal community find just the opposite. It is helpful, then, to examine the ideological drives of these communities and determine how their ideologies affect characterizations of property, authorship, and ownership of intellectual creation and thereby inform their interpretation of intellectual property law as it develops in response to the Internet.

Controlling Ideology in Cyberspace

Academicians in humanistic studies and participants on the Internet share ideological beliefs in support of broad access to information. In addition, law professionals, as well as academic humanists who use the Internet and digitized materials in their teaching and research, have been influenced by the effects of technology, as well as ideology of the Internet community. Early work by Jay David Bolter in *Writing Space,* Richard Lanham in *Hypertext,* and George Landow in *The Digital Word* introduces concepts regarding electronic text that make clear how digitized text epitomizes social construction and challenges traditional views of ownership in the products of intellectual creation when applied to true hypertextual creations such as multiply linked websites. Such analyses of hypertext have accomplished two tasks: to illustrate the impact of hypertextual writing on thinking and creating and to illustrate that even in print text, intellectual creation is hypertextual in nature. Bolter notes that electronic writing emphasizes the impermanence of text by creating a new writing surface that changes each time a new individual influences the work (3). Rather than treating text as a discrete map of an individual's thoughts, the new technology mandates that text be treated as a network of verbal ideas. Hypertext is a writing space with an erasable surface (55) that responds to multiple influences from many individuals who continuously change the ideas represented there. Many individuals create a "final" written text out of multiple influences, making questionable any given single author's authority in his or her "individual" work. As such, the erasable writing surface of hypertext, almost allegorical in nature, calls for the end of authority in individual works (5, 55, 153). Ideas of others inevitably influence the hypertext author, but ideas in print, oral presentation, television, movies, art, music, and all other forms of communication also are created from a societal web of intertextual thought (163). Richard Lanham questions whether ownership of intellectual "property" has ever been possible, whether in print or digital form, and notes that the long-held assumption of exclusive ownership has been in error.

George Landow compares the influences of hypertext on the concept of authorship in print media with those in digital expression and points out that the costs and conditions of print technology create concepts of originality and authorial property in a way that digital text does not (6). Because print materials in the forms of books, journals, and printed pages are contained in a static "final" physical form, the thoughts within them are seemingly complete and exclusive to the author or authors whose names are printed on the covers. In contrast, the ease of manipulation of digital text in its cut-and-paste capability makes it less likely for any one author to make exclusive claim to an "original" idea (12–13). In an address to participants in the 1999 Conference on College Composition and Communication's Intellectual Property Caucus, Jay Bolter noted the problem with the early claims about hypertext in his own work and in that of Landow, Lanham, and others. He pointed out that widespread use of hypertext has not actually moved us as a culture to lessen the authority of the author, noting that if this were the case, our notions of copyright would be changing as a result. Bolter commented that, in fact, the opposite is happening as individuals and corporations are becoming vigilant in their pursuit of trademark and copyright protections, asserting claims that in many cases are much stronger than those made for print. He points to the fact that we have to argue so vigorously for fair use in the digital age as evidence that copyright is becoming stringent. It may be that the nature of digitized material, because it is so fluid, is the fundamental cause of difficulties in applying intellectual property law.

The use of digital texts produces new problems with intellectual property law that stem from the technology's refocusing of thought on the concepts of ownership, authorial control, and reader access (Landow 16). "Electronic text and copyright are steering a collision course at almost every point" (Lanham 134). That all texts borrow from each other changes the whole idea behind copyright (Landow 1) because when text is no longer fixed, there is no more assumption that the work is final in a completed form. Even "our ethics of quotation and the stylistic formulas that embody it, is called into question by the electronic media" (19).

Despite the influence of digitized text and the Internet, and a strong ideological basis of belief in constructionist thought, the community of academicians in humanistic studies is somewhat divided in that its purposes and focuses are dual. Academicians have strong interests as users of intellectual property, in particular, to ensure that copyrighted work is available for educational purposes to advance the development of knowledge. In addition, most academicians are also creators of intellectual products in hard copy as well as digital forms. Although pedagogically speaking, many instructors focus on process orientations in their classrooms, most prepare students for workplace settings where they will focus their efforts on the intellectual product and its economic usefulness to the employer who hires them as contract employees, the company that employs them, or the buyers of the product. Workplace creators and their (often corporate) employers are interested in preserving their right to benefit from the intellectual product they have created; thus, the ideological stance taken by creators, whether academic or not, would be squarely protectionist in nature. Argumentation surrounding copyright from this viewpoint parallels that of authors' rights in general and is treated in the great majority of legal handbooks on intellectual property. But even creators with protectionist interests work in circumstances where they collaborate with others to produce intellectual expressions, and as multiple authorship of digitized information becomes more and more common, establishing who retains rights to use and sell intellectual works will become more difficult.

The collaborative nature of both the workplace and the classroom is well documented, and its effects are considered appropriate for furthering accepted goals of these writing forums. A number of researchers have reported that because collaboration is in force in workplace settings, its impact should be considered in how we understand the development of knowledge in society. Research in this area explains the importance of the discursive "conversation" among scientists, lawyers, medical technicians, engineers, and many others for developing knowledge in their respective fields and strongly supports the collaborative process both in workplace and in educational settings. The dominant constructionist viewpoint in humanistic studies provides support for collaboration by encouraging negotiation. Like the communal negotiation that occurs on the Internet, collaboration is nonfoundational in nature; there is no assumption that parties will locate preexisting creative products either through access to the environment or within themselves but that intellectual products will be developed through a melding of contributions from members of the group. Collaborative acts require interdependence; thus, the act of creating focuses on a community of creators rather than one independent author. Collaboration requires a negotiation toward consensus among parties to the creation of a work; the process of negotiation may be lengthy, frustrating, and difficult but opens possibilities for considering minority viewpoints.

In supporting an ideological paradigm that privileges the collaborative process of creation, the academic humanist community also establishes representative viewpoints regarding authority and access to knowledge creation. Proponents of collaboration favor knowledge creation that provides egalitarian access by individuals with a variety of viewpoints; consideration of multiple influences is encouraged. The way a community defines and characterizes the concept of authorship is fundamentally based on its ideological stance toward ownership and property and what that stance means for controlling the creation, development, and dissemination of knowledge. A close look at these issues will make clear that ideological views of property can have an important pragmatic impact on our rights as users and producers of knowledge. Where the Internet and academic humanist communities view authorship and control of intellectual products as community-based, the legal community follows a foundational, Romantic ideology and treats intellectual products as property, thus placing control of information in the hands of few but powerful individual and corporate entities.

Legal Interpretations of "Property"

A community's ideological belief forms the basis for how the community defines property; differing definitions of property lead to different interpretations of the intellectual property law, thus very different conclusions about how information and knowledge production should be controlled. Conflicts over rights to intellectual products usually arise between creators and users of intellectual work or between more than one creator claiming rights to the same intellectual work; the issues driving these conflicts are usually economic in nature. Although the constitutional intellectual property provision is based on policy considerations and its function was intended only to regulate how intellectual work is treated, because courts rarely consider policy cases regarding conflicts over intellectual products, most lawyers and judges mistakenly treat intellectual work as property, thus the common name "intellectual property." The framers of the Constitution developed the intellectual property provision to maintain a balance between the public's need for information and authors' rights to benefit from the work they produce. The public needs to use the information held within an intellectual product in a way that will benefit society by being able to access ideas in order to build knowledge; an author needs to protect property from theft, to be compensated for creating intellectual property, and to prohibit unauthorized changes to a work in such a way as to harm his or her name and reputation. Because the legal system is adversarial, proponents of these dichotomous positions rarely take a middle ground in arguing for support of one side or the other. Instead, legislators negotiate conflicting policy issues when they create statutory law, while courts interpret the resulting statutory laws in the court system. It is important to understand the potential effects of imbalance between these two sets of concerns.

Judges' and lawyers' constructed ideologies influence the way they consider intellectual property; differing ideologies in law derive different interpretations of property. Whether copyright is interpreted as a natural-law property right or a statutory grant of authors' limited monopolies in their work is central to differences in characterization of property. The proprietary view claims that authors have rights of ownership in works; application of proprietary natural law derives from the concept of "moral rights," which ensures that authors maintain the right to benefit from the work they have created, often called the right to work by the "sweat of the brow." This premise is based on the common law of copyright developed in England.[1]

The statutory law promulgated by the 1976 Copyright Act, on the other hand, maintains that authors should benefit from their work but simultaneously emphasizes the need for right of public access to authors' expressions in order to aid society by furthering learning. Based on the concept that societal knowledge is developed incrementally, influenced by prior knowledge, the statutory law is intended to regulate authors' control over their work. To ensure that knowledge be made available for public use to "further science [knowledge] and the useful arts," the statute assigns authors the right to *limited* monopolies in their work. The limitations created in section 107 of the 1976 Copyright Act, the "fair use" rulings, set limits on the duration that material can be kept from the public and make provisions for fair use of materials to allow access to protected expressions within the term of their copyright. The distinctions between the goals of copyright as applied in common law cases and as construed in the statute are significant. The common law serves to create proprietary rights in the work itself, in the embodiment of the ideas as well as in the expression of the work. As I noted in chapter 2, the 1976 statutory law severs rights in the ideas of the work from the expression of those ideas and protects only the expression. This makes clear, of course, that copyright in the expression is subject to fair use exceptions and that authors' rights are not proprietary in nature.

The distinctions between common law proprietary rights and the rights provided by statute can be clarified through a very brief historical consideration of the concept of property ownership. The concept of common law property arises from a time in which ownership was possible only in a tangible entity such as a cow or bale of hay. Owners maintained their proprietary rights through exclusive physical possession of these material entities. With these proprietary rights came the right to transfer property to another individual through contract, gift, or will. Once an owner transferred rights in property, that property was no longer in the physical possession of its original owner but in the possession of the transferee. Inherent in common law proprietorship was the concept that only one owner could maintain possession of property at one time.

Early in the history of intellectual property, authors created and transcribed intellectual products embodied in verses of poetry, musical arrangements, and prose texts and maintained them as single physical entities in the forms of handwritten books, sheets of music, and pages of poetry. At this time, before the development and use of the printing press, copying was painstakingly difficult and time-consuming; thus, making copies of intellectual products was rare. Common law property law was almost as effective a legal device for the settlement of dispute over newly created intellectual property as it was for cattle and other tangible items. Once an author transferred an intellectual product to another, it became the exclusive property of that owner in the same way that one would possess a tangible object, for intellectual products were, in essence, physical entities.[2]

After the development of the printing press, the intellectual product became less tangible. Publishers could easily make copies and disseminate them to many; thus, ownership was no longer limited because no one individual could maintain exclusive physical control over a single work. At this point, the stationers, the early version of publishers, entered the picture. The value of a work no longer arose in its worth to a single buyer but in its popularity among multiple buyers. Stationers paid authors flat sums for their works and then printed, distributed, and collected fees for multiple copies sold to willing buyers. Authors transferred the rights in their work to publishers who effectively retained the right to benefit from copy of the work; thus, the concept of copyright as it is often used today, was created.

Where common law emphasizes ownership of the work itself, current statutory copyright law focuses on the separation of the right to the expression of the work from the ideas within the work. To encourage access to the ideas of a work will encourage learning and advance knowledge in society, the statutory goal. Common law copyright emphasis in the concept of ownership effectively prohibits the publics' access to the ideas in a work; the term *ownership* denotes the right to exclude others from the use or access to that which is owned; thus, when a court applies common law natural rights, it effectively nullifies the legislative act created in the 1976 statute, which made common law applications to copyright obsolete. In applying common law, courts that forgo the language of the statute implicitly give authors exclusive rights to the information they produce.

Some legal analysts who are driven by the same positivist notions of authorship that supported common law treatment of intellectual products as property misconstrue the 1976 copyright statute to argue that it supports the same "authors' rights" arguments. Often, lawyers who take this kind of protectionist stance toward authors' monopolies attempt to weaken the fair use exceptions by construing the language narrowly (Patterson and Lindberg 9). The suggested guidelines for fair use developed by ad hoc committees during legislative considerations leading to the 1976 act were highly restrictive to public access. Where the committee offered "safe" specifics in quantifying the number of words or paragraphs that could be copied without infringement, they actually created limits on the actual statement of the law by developing minimum standards of fair use that are viewed by copyright holders as well as risk-wary users as maximum allowable use (9). This kind of strict construction furthers the common law goal of proprietorship by assigning ownership to copyright holders in the form of nearly exclusive control of the intellectual product. Statutory construction of this kind that supports a protectionist ideology disregards the policy behind the constitutional provision as Congress explicitly wrote it in the 1976 Copyright Act. Its intent was to support public access to intellectual creations in order to advance societally influenced knowledge.

Legal analysts such as L. Ray Patterson and Stanley Lindberg, who take a contrasting ideology in support of public access, view this construction as restrictive and argue that it "conflicts with the basic policies and principles that inform copyright—thus serving mainly to intimidate users and inhibit the advancement of knowledge" (9). Public access— "users' rights"—proponents argue that the fundamental purpose of the copyright statute is to advance society by making knowledge available to all citizens:

> The primary purpose of copyright—as stated explicitly by the framers of the Constitution and subsequently interpreted by the federal courts and Congress—is to promote the public welfare by the advancement of knowledge. With the specific intent of encouraging the production and distribution of new works for the public, copyright provides incentive for creators by granting them exclusive rights to reproduce and distribute their work. But these rights are subject to important limitations—nearly all of them related to the basic purpose of advancing knowledge for the general welfare of society.(2)

As I noted earlier, the policy goal of the law that treats copyright is stated in the intellectual property clause of the Constitution. The promotion of knowledge is the primary focus of the clause; the limited protection of authors' rights in their work, necessary to this purpose. Promotion of knowledge is accomplished *by* securing limited rights to authors. The limitation to authors is in the duration that they retain their rights, the intention being to create a public domain of works to be used by the public. Proponents of the public's right of access to authors' work point out that it was later, in the enactment of the fair use provision of section 107 of the 1976 Copyright Act, that Congress made the constitutional intent to support public access to copyrighted work even more clear.

The basic ideology that drives proponents of the users' rights stance (as opposed to that of legal analysts who argue that authors' rights to economic benefit from their work is primary) is the belief that access to information is necessary to the growth and positive development of society, and this right to access overrides that of the right to individual economic benefit. "The key to appreciating copyright is that it is given grudgingly. There is something in the free enterprise system that doesn't like a monopoly, and the authors of the Constitution seemed to share that view" (Kleinman 24). But "while copyright in one sense is a statute, it also is a constitutional principle," because ". . . copyright, as a public policy, is almost as integral to our own government as is freedom of the press. Moreover, it is the only public policy extant that is designed specifically to promote the creation of new concepts, ideas, and theories for society, as well as to encourage their dissemination" (Henry 17). The users' rights concept, then, emphasizes the societal need for information.

These divergent ideologies that drive differing interpretations of copyright produce contrary treatments of the concept of proprietorship in intellectual products. The protectionist viewpoint focuses on the exclusivity of ownership in the same way that the common law concept of property, by necessity, made an owner's right to a tangible good exclusive from others. The users' rights viewpoint, on the other hand, maintains a two-point position: (1) the intellectual product is ephemeral and can be contained in more than one place at one time, and (2) new knowledge is created on the basis of the existence of prior knowledge. The users' rights viewpoint supports society's interest in accessing the intellectual product; it advances the belief that no one in society should be allowed to maintain totally exclusive ownership in intellectual products. This stance also provides an answer for how to adjust intellectual property law to account for the new character of digitized information and the collaborative development and sharing of information that occurs through the Internet.

Understanding proprietorship becomes more complicated by the 1976 statute, which makes clear that ideas are severable from the expression of those ideas (the intellectual product) and that only the expression is protected under copyright. Protectionists argue that since the ideas are what motivate new knowledge, limited access to the expression should not hamper the constitutional policy. But users' rights proponents point out that since the ideas of a work are contained in its expression, the only means to access them is through access to the expression. In addition, society has an interest in the ability to copy passages of other works in order to quote original authors in their own words and for purposes of parody to express dissenting ideas.

The real crux of the conflict for the protectionists is the question of who benefits economically from intellectual products: they want to ensure that copyright holders retain all the economic benefits in their products. The common law concept of exclusive ownership and a narrow reading of the copyright act provide the most protection for economic rights in copyright holders because it is exclusively prohibitive of use by others.

Users' rights proponents have little economic interest in intellectual products but are concerned that the economic argument could prohibit societal access to intellectual products and thus hamper public development of new knowledge and act as censorship. The problem, they point out, is that in order to publish their work, authors transfer their economic rights in the intellectual product to publishers who then control the dissemination of information (knowledge) to the public. It is not the economic question that worries users' rights proponents but publishers' powerful control over all new knowledge created. Even more alarming, rich individuals and corporations with massive corporate holdings, such as Bill Gates and the Disney Corporation, are buying the rights to control huge amounts of intellectual products: information. They maintain powerful legal staffs to ensure that this information is licensed only to those users they deem desirable and only for purposes of which they approve. Corporate information holders have the power to use the law to affect cultural development and public speech. "In the current climate, intellectual property laws often operate to stifle dialogic practice in the public sphere, preventing us from using the most powerful, prevalent, and accessible cultural forms to express alternative visions of social worlds" (Coombe, *Cultural Life* 42). When restrictive interpretations of the law limit public dialogue by narrowing access to what *was* societally influenced information, the voice of the people is squelched and only corporate entities and wealthy individuals who contain large amounts of cultural information can participate in making the reality that is our culture. "Too broad a set of intellectual property rights gives one set of persons potential control over how that 'created' reality can be interpreted. In other words, it can give them control over what the world *means*" (Gordon in Coombe, *Cultural Life* 51). A community's ideological stance toward intellectual property in law has important implications; applying these two greatly conflicting stances produces very different interpretations of the constitutional policy behind the intellectual property statute.

The Romantic concept of authorship has been replaced with a postmodern view that questions the assumption that authorship connotes personal property and ownership (Jaszi, "Toward a Theory of Copyright"; Woodmansee and Jaszi, "Law of Texts"). The concept of "authorship" is derived from a literary background of foundational belief in the locus of "Truth" and knowledge in the individual (Jaszi, "Toward a Theory of Copyright" 455), but authorship "is a culturally, politically, economically, and socially constructed category rather than a real or natural one" (459). In the social constructionist view adopted by educators in humanistic studies and participants of the Internet community, no work stands alone but builds from prior knowledge and insight. But when courts, researchers, individuals, and corporate copyright holders apply the common law ideal, they treat the intellectual product like the exclusive property of the individual creator. The common law, based on eighteenth-century thought and developed within an eighteenth-century contextual setting, assumes that authors create in isolation. This concept of authorship has been uncritically accepted in the legal field: "The whole structure . . . is grounded on an uncritical belief in the existence of a distinct and privileged category of activity that generates products of special social value, entitling the practitioners (the 'authors') to unique rewards" (466).

Even the concept of "genius" as it relates to definitions of property and ownership of knowledge affects characterizations of knowledge and property. Under the concept of genius, novel information in literature is provided by the muse or divine dictation, giving the author a presumptive special power and a special right to the knowledge he or she "produces." In turn, this assumption supports the concept of ownership in property based on a belief in the genius as uniquely endowed in a way that few others are. The genius then maintains a special status and special authority in the work created (Woodmansee 427). The concept of authority is two-pronged. The author's unique position, enlightened by the muse and given the status of genius, (1) conveys authority in the validity of his/her intellectual "creation" and (2) maintains exclusive control over the creation; thus the power, or "authority," to prohibit others from its use. Ownership of work (property) is a necessary precondition of authorship (Jaszi, "Toward a Theory of Copyright" 431) and the status conveyed by the Romantic concept of "author" provides both.

Academicians in humanistic studies, participants in the Internet community, some legal scholars, and others who ascribe to constructionist ideology affirm that all members of society should influence the development of the knowledge that controls that society. Arguments by scholars in humanistic studies demonstrate how important it is that we note the negative effects of a diminished public domain and that we treat intellectual products respectfully but openly, furthering support of public access (Gurak). Works that treat intellectual property from humanistic studies perspectives question the role of the author as sole owner of knowledge and of intellectual works, illustrate the many ways in which the restrictive lines that define authorship are melting away (Latchaw and Galin), and point out that electric forums such as MOOs and MUDs, by their very nature, create collaborative "authorship" of the texts within them (Kolko). This work supports the concept that the condition of authorship assigns ownership to the community rather than to one individual; thus, control over knowledge is nonexclusive. The result is the dispersal of power throughout the community rather than locating it in a privileged few.

7

The New Millennium
and Controlling Voices

Intellectual expression is always a conglomeration of the ideas and influences of individuals, societal organizations, and community ideologies, but digitization of text and Internet communication both intensify and make conspicuous the merger of many individuals' ideas and expressions. Understanding the effect of digitized text and Internet communication provides all the more reason for fighting for society's interests in securing public access to information, especially for educators in humanistic studies. First, to accept that intellectual expression is intangible negates application of the common law concept of property, which applies only to tangible entities; intangible intellectual products can be simultaneously controlled by more than one creator. Second, digitization can change the character of information so that its ideas and their expression are inseparable. Under these circumstances, when a court grants an individual creator exclusive right to intellectual products, it inhibits access to the ideas in intellectual work and defeats the purpose of the intellectual property statute in furthering the progress of learning in society.

Throughout the history of intellectual property argument, the proprietary focus has been on the expression of ideas and not on the ideas themselves, but the ideas have always been considered the collective property of humanity (Barlow). Digitized information illustrates metaphorically and actually the implausibility of exclusive ownership in intellectual products and casts doubt that authorship should produce ownership and, thus, exclusive control.

The conclusion that digitized information is commingled seems unchallenged in the Internet community; evidence that information should be shared is overwhelming. This attitude is prevalent, for example, in the choices made in programming and using the software that makes electronic mail technology possible. E-mail programming allows readers to easily copy text into their own documents for comment. Internet software also allows users simple and quick means to copy and send whole messages from original writers to new recipients with e-mail accounts. The conventions of most e-mail lists are such that participants expect their messages to be distributed further beyond the original list. World Wide Web applications also encourage free use of web materials. Typical commands allow users to access and copy web page source code in two simple steps, as well as locate and copy graphics and sound; users can also transfer whole graphic, sound, or text files easily and quickly. Whether the ability to copy information easily is grounds for doing so is not at issue here, but most participants on the Internet presume that the functions of these Internet applications help define the parameters of acceptable use. The common beliefs within the Internet community are that "[e]lectronic information seems to resist ownership" (Lanham 19) and that the Internet should be used as a means to convey information quickly and freely, with the benefits going to the general community of users. The implication is that from this ideological standpoint, copyright law should not hamper the commonly accepted notion that information should be freely accessible, with authority to control information given to the general public of users.

Internet participants' view of authority also influences their estimation of property. Copyright holders claim rights in intellectual products on the basis of their authorship (or as owners of rights transferred by authors). Authorship is "the most resonant, of the foundational concepts associated with the Anglo-American copyright doctrine" (Jaszi, "Toward a Theory of Copyright" 455). But the dominant views in the academic humanist and Internet communities indicate that authorship never wholly resides in one individual, but that the ideas that an author generates are socially constructed and developed from influences of prior knowledge: that is, "authorship . . . is a culturally, politically, economically, and socially constructed category rather than a real or natural one" (459). In theoretical application of this view, no one author can ever retain the right to exclusive control of an intellectual product.

The constructionist view makes this concept an even stronger proposition, since its basic assumption is that all ideas are produced through collective influences. A community that sees benefits in collaboration acknowledges the need for access to creative products in order to enable collaboration, since new knowledge is created under the influence of other knowledge (Anderson in Barrett 109). If we truly support participatory democracy as a nation, we must support interpretations of intellectual property law that enable collaborative influences of all citizens, since participation in the conversation of society is participation in the creation of what we are as a culture. Accessing and creating knowledge not only aid an individual in assimilating into a community but ensure that the individual will also have a voice that influences the determination of what the community becomes. In addition, "[k]nowledge is the essence of public policy making. Who has it and who lacks it determines what public policies will be" (Henry 2). It "influences public policies at least as much as public policies affect patterns of knowledge" (1). It is important to proponents of a social constructionist philosophy, then, that on a practical level the public has access to information that affects the policies that, in turn, influence the laws that govern the behavior of all individuals in society.

Intellectual property law was conceived within the outdated view of Romantic authorship, but a revised view of authorship within a constructionist stance accounts for the effects of digitized information and Internet communication. It also supports the need for egalitarian ownership of knowledge by all participants of a learning community. But courts will defeat the egalitarian goals of academicians in humanistic studies and of members of the Internet community if they continue to apply foundational, Romantic views of authorship. A prominent aspect of the traditional concept of authority is its ability to create status, which in turn ultimately places the power to control access to information in the hands of the status holder. Under common law, the status of those who held the title of author provided them with exclusive rights to pronounce "Truth." They maintained power by controlling knowledge and choosing its eventual recipients. Historically, with the characterization of author came the special status of genius that encouraged special treatment of the author as one who had the ability to create knowledge for the whole of society (Jaszi, "On the Author Effect" 35). The result is to place power over information in the hands of a few "chosen" individuals.

Copyright Power

A synthesis of the issues surrounding copyright law that are most significant for academicians in humanistic studies produces revealing conclusions regarding the competing ideologies in the legal community as they apply to intellectual property law. "Discussions of copyright doctrine tend to assume the importance of 'authorship' as a privileged category of human enterprise, rather than to examine where this notion arose or how it has influenced the law" (Jaszi, "Toward a Theory of Copyright" 455). "[C]opyright received a constructed idea of 'authorship' from literary and artistic culture and . . . this 'authorship construct' has been mobilized in legal discourse" (456) to the extent that the multiple functions of "authorship" create incoherence in copyright doctrine (457). The legal community's acceptance of the Romantic concept of authorship conflicts with the dominant social constructionist view in humanistic studies. The unusual power and persistence of the law's foundational concept of authorship are the specific locus of contradiction between public access to and private control over imaginative creations (457). But the concept of authorship has been accepted in intellectual property law: "the whole structure . . . is grounded on an uncritical belief in the existence of a distinct and privileged category of activity, that generates products of special social value, entitling the practitioners (the 'authors') to unique rewards" (466). Very few academicians would question authors' rights to benefit from their work, but to extend that benefit to *exclusive* control inhibits the public's access to information and the development of knowledge by participants in the community dialogue. This result is counter to the community goals of furthering egalitarian access to the intellectual product and to the process of creating knowledge as well.

In addition, when courts interpret copyright laws on the basis of a presumption of Romantic authorship—thus, authority and control over intellectual products—they potentially restrict free speech; individuals cannot speak about what they cannot access. The concept of rights based in the special status created by a Romantic view of authorship is diluted when those rights are transferred to publishers, whose fundamental interest is economic.

Historically, the Stationers' Copyright protected booksellers (Patterson and Lindberg 21), and today, although they may not use it, publishers still maintain the power to censor expression, since the ability to disseminate information is in their hands. In the early British history of copyright from which we have developed our own law, the stationers' (early publishers) desire for legal copyright coincided with the government's need to gain control over "the dangerous possibilities of the printed word" (23). The stationers supported control because regulation also provided protection of their copyright, but the stationers' copyright became a tool of censorship (126). Public cries against censorship were finally answered, against the crown's wishes.

Significantly, publishers, by necessity, are motivated by economic interests rather than interests in public welfare. The 1976 Copyright Act includes the fair use exceptions as a means to defeat the possibility of censorship and to make clear the policy of the statute in the promotion of learning, because "[w]hile copyright in one sense is a statute, it also is a constitutional principle" (Henry 17). The purpose of copyright is clear:

[C]opyright, as a public policy, is almost as integral to our own government as is freedom of the press. Moreover, it is the only public policy extant which is designed specifically to promote the creation of new concepts, ideas, and theories for society, as well as to encourage their dissemination. (17)

Copyright law can nevertheless be misused as a method for censorship. The result of restrictive interpretation of the fair use exceptions is censorship. "In the current climate, intellectual property laws stifle dialogic practices, preventing us from using the most powerful, prevalent, and accessible cultural forms to express identity, community, and difference" (Coombe, "Objects of Property" 277). Congress intended that the fair use exceptions guarantee that copyrighted materials could be used as the subject of commentary and parody in addition to personal and educational uses, but protecting economic rights in the copy has been the main focus of recent battles over these issues. Rosemary Coombe illustrates the typical conflict between the public's right to create parody for the purpose of political comment and the copyright holder's right to reap all economic benefits from the copy. She uses an example from popular culture in an instance in which a group of ghetto entrepreneurs in New York City created a t-shirt design depicting an African American version of the comedy television cartoon character Bart Simpson. The parodic Simpson figure was depicted wearing an Afro and a dashiki, and displayed a clenched fist to indicate an expression in favor of power in the African American community. Coombe explains that the copyright holders of the Bart Simpson image were successful in a suit for infringement but, she points out, equally successful in stifling free speech. When a cultural icon gathers meaning because of its reception and reaction from the community, its connotation for society is socially constructed. Coombe argues that economic interests in the intellectual product should not outweigh the value of that icon for public commentary. Society is so culturally inundated with signs and slogans that they make up a large part of our lives ("Objects of Property" 283) upon which we base political expression. People "engage in meaning making to adapt signs, texts, and images to their own agendas" ("Objects of Property" 285). Coombe explains the importance of culturally influenced forms of expression to society's makeup:

What I'm suggesting here is that intellectual property laws may define use of the optimal cultural condition for the dialogic practice. By objectifying and reifying cultural forms—freezing the connotations of signs and symbols and fencing off fields of cultural meaning with "no trespassing" signs—intellectual property laws may enable certain forms of political practice and constrain others. ("Objects of Property" 288)

A recent example of the misuse of the copyright statute to inhibit parody is a situation in which copyright holders brought suits against rap singers for graphics used in music videos that were "copies" of the seals and symbols of local police departments. Coincidentally, the lyrics of these targeted music videos were not only uncomplimentary but even somewhat threatening to the police. Although not encouraging violent acts against members of law enforcement, opposing legal analysts point out the chilling effect of these lawsuits on free speech. In an earlier work, I argue that where the First Amendment assures that we have a right to voice our ideas, assert conflicting views from which new thought is derived, and criticize thought and action of powerful forces in society, fair use provides a means to access the information upon which our opinions are based. Without this interdependency of fair use and the First Amendment that provides an exception to copyright, "free speech would be, at best, inhibited and in some cases, eliminated altogether" (Herrington, "Interdependency" 125).

John Shelton Lawrence provides an interesting view of the copyright protection afforded a large and powerful corporate entity against individuals whose work provides unflattering political parody. He describes a case in which Ariel Dorfman and Armand Mattelart produced a parody of Disney's material in the form of a cartoon-style book entitled *How to Read Donald Duck*. The book is extremely unflattering to Disney, pointing out, among other things, the aggressive nature by which the Disney corporation collects wealth and its cavalier production of bigoted depictions of peoples of less powerful ethnic groups. At issue was that *How to Read Donald Duck* includes parodic images of characters created by Disney, which are attributed with ironic speech characterizing Dorfman and Mattelart's critical view. The authors claimed that the substance of the views depicted is inseparable from the use of the images. In an effort to prohibit further production and distribution of the work, the Disney corporation claimed that the authors violated copyright. In this instance, as in those mentioned above, Disney attempted to use the copyright law as a means to inhibit free speech. Not only is the use of copyright law to promote censorship contrary to the goals supported by the dominant views of members of the community of academic humanists who support egalitarian access to the dialogic process, it is also contrary to the views of a number of legal analysts who follow a paradigm that favors protection of the public domain. This kind of misuse of copyright law to inhibit free speech may become more common; fear of infringement resulting from widespread copying and transferring information on the Internet has resulted in recent restrictive protectionist changes in the intellectual property law (NET Act, Sonny Bono Copyright Extension Act).

A further complication is that authors rarely retain control over the intellectual products that they create but transfer to publishers the right to distribute information. When publishers hold the rights to copy and disseminate information, they also retain the power to control who can and cannot gain access to knowledge and to determine which knowledge is worthy of dissemination. The outcome is that effectively all of society's knowledge is placed under the control of a very powerful select few. This situation, of course, runs contrary to the goals inherent in an ideology that supports egalitarian access to and control of knowledge. Additionally significant for the copyright law is that the legal construct that supports the "moral rights" doctrine, that authors have rights to their intellectual products created by "the sweat of the brow," is defeated when creators transfer exclusive rights to publishers. Ultimately, this legal construction protects publishers' rather than authors' rights, thereby nullifying the "sweat of the brow" argument.

To some extent the Romantic view of status that accompanies authorship continues today by necessity. A particular problem for academicians whose careers lie in the ability to publish is that the currency of the academic world is intellectual. For academicians, job security and promotions depend on the quantity of works that they can publish and on the status of the journals and publishing houses that handle them. Status and authorship are still conflated in the academic world, despite inconsistency with the ideological goals of the academic communities in humanistic studies. At present, the status/authorship characterization of intellectual property is inconsistent with the dominant ideological goals of the community but consistent with a Romantic view of authorship for purposes of copyright. The joining of the concepts of status and authorship marks inconsistencies in ideologic approach that should be considered when a stance toward copyright is being developed.

To complicate matters further, the concept of originality is the basis for publication of work. The social constructionist view denies that total originality in work is possible since, in this view, no ideas are ever original but are developed from prior knowledge. The introduction of digital communication complicates these issues even further. Richard Lanham wonders how writing in hypertext will affect publication status when questions arise as to who owns a hypertext and the attached subtexts (20). Lanham postulates that we will have to reconsider questions of originality and the system of promotion and tenure based on this concept (134). Definitions of intellectual property ownership, then, become difficult to pin down because claims to ownership in intangible, commingled intellectual products are tenuous at best. If ownership requires exclusive control over the entity claimed as property, it may be doubtful that any one individual could claim exclusive ownership in electronic data, since writers have limited control over what part of an intellectual product is theirs and what belongs to another contributor of knowledge.

Many members of academic humanist and Internet communities favor open access to knowledge and characterize intellectual production as the intangible creative construct of the whole of society. Since authorship is influenced by the community as a whole, no one individual can claim exclusive control of the intellectual product; thus, authority lies in a negotiated consensus that takes into consideration the disparate views of all participants in society rather than placing special status in a select "genius" of authorship. Authority to contribute to the creation of knowledge and, thus, the power to determine the framework of society lies in the hands of all members of society. These egalitarian goals are forwarded when access to that knowledge is nonexclusively controlled. Educators in humanistic studies and others who are interested in ensuring free speech and a healthy public domain should enter the discussion in order to influence development of intellectual property law in response to the challenges of new technology.

Digitizing Copyright

Many legal researchers claim that the current law is inadequate to treat the new issues that arise as a result of the change in communication technology. Nicholas Negroponte calls the current intellectual property law "a Gutenberg artifact . . . [which] will probably have to break down completely before it is converted" (58). Law professor Pamela Samuelson states that "there is also a growing recognition . . . of the potential of digital media to change the face of intellectual property law" ("Digital Media" 324). According to Richard Lanham, "[e]lectronic text and copyright are steering a collision course at almost every point" (134), and in George Landow's view, it is apparent that digital texts produce new problems with law, since there are new problems of ownership, authorial control, and reader access (16).

The technology produces new ways to deal with text that legislators did not consider in the original drafting of the statue. The 1976 Copyright Act requires that information be *tangible* and perceivable, that is, readable by the recipients. Many adjudicators question whether the very act of reading digital information, because it requires a translation, is in itself an act of copying the work, thus, a violation of copyright. In addition, Samuelson lists six characteristics of digitized expression that will cause difficulties with the protections provided by intellectual property law:

> (1) the ease with which the works in digital form can be replicated, (2) the ease with which they can be transmitted, (3) the ease with which they can be modified and manipulated, (4) the equivalence

in digital form, (5) the compactness of works in digital form, and (6) the capacity they have for creating new methods for searching digital space and linking works together. ("Digital Media" 324)

John Perry Barlow also points to how difficult it is to protect digitized text. He questions how it is possible to protect property within media that allow easy and infinite copying and that can be instantaneously distributed all over the world. Samuelson notes, "What makes works in digital form so much more threatening is that the same technology one needs to use the digital work is the technology that can be used to make multiple copies of the work—and even more frighteningly, can be used to produce 'perfect' copies" ("Digital Media" 326). In addition, work that, in the past, might not be transferred because it was either too deep or too broad (like an encyclopedia) could now be copied exactly and in a matter of minutes. Many authors, publishers, and legal analysts who favor interpretations of copyright law from a protectionist stance fear that the economic power of authors and publishers will be harmed, since authorized sale of work can be so easily bypassed (Clapes, Bush, Simon, Galler, Neitzke).

When producers intermingle separately authored texts, graphics, video, and sound bytes, they commingle authorship in a way that the law does not consider. The pragmatic implications resulting from the use of multimedia technology are staggering for multimedia producers who feel that the market is suffering from intellectual property laws not adequate to meet the needs of copyrighted materials in digital form. They note that demands for copyright fees are unrealistic and that it is unreasonable for ASCAP and BMI (licensers of use of broad collections of works) to charge for the use of all the works in a collection when only one or a very few are used. Using licensed work creates a particular hardship when multimedia producers have to pay licensing fees even for content that is not used (Foremski 218). It is very difficult to create a noninfringing multimedia work:

> A would-be multimedia producer must obtain permission from scattered writers, musicians, photographers, and artists at a cost that is impossible to predict. Any rights holder may veto an entire production simply by refusing to grant a license. Under such pressure the producer may choose to use a different source, to erase the holder's voice or image from the new production, or to infringe copyrighted work and accept possible litigation as a business cost. (Ocampo and Shellenhase 71)

The question remains whether copyright claims still apply to individual works when all the sources are combined. The combination of many sources that make up the final product is sufficiently different from each original source to make an argument that only the multimedia producer has a claim in the work. "A collective work can warrant copyright protection distinct from the copyrights of the individual works of which it is composed" (Cavazos and Morin 50), but this characterization of the intellectual product unfairly denies compensation to the original contributors of all the constituent pieces.

Publishers, a huge block of copyright holders in America, experience additional problems that arise as a result of digitized communication. In the past, individuals who wanted to contribute to the conversation of the community by way of text had to submit work to be approved, bought, copied, and disseminated by publishers. Publishers' decisions about what to publish were based on preferences developed as a result of formal education in liberal arts fields and on the work's potential for economic success. Publishing in print form is an expensive proposition. Costs incurred include those for paper, ink, printing, layout, artwork, binding, storing, shipping, and the salaries of employees. In addition to publishing staff such as reviewers and editors, publishers must pay attorneys who contract with authors and any other subcontractor used to complete publications.

The economic barriers to self-publication in print are difficult to overcome, but digital communication has made it not only possible but relatively easy for individuals to publish their own materials on the Internet through e-mail and the World Wide Web. "When you make a public blackboard you make everyone a publisher or broadcaster of text" (Rheingold 113). The Web is the public blackboard that is beginning to erase the need for publishers to control the dissemination of information. Today everyone who has access to the Web and has the ability to use it can be a publisher, thereby stripping the publishing monopoly from the hands of the few and dispersing it into the control of many. The result is that a massive amount of information is available at the touch of a keypad.

The Web's availability for publication has created an influx of published materials that have bypassed "certification" of the publishing process. Materials published on the Web are accessible without direct cost to the user. Although much of what is published is of low quality, many digital documents are useful and contain ideas that contribute to developing knowledge in a variety of fields. These materials are easily and quickly accessible and are free for public use, an enticing combination for readers. Although the accessibility of digital text is no real threat to publishers at present, the potential for diminishing their ability to bargain for new material does exist.

The greatest current threat to print publishers is the continuing convention among members of the Internet community to copy and post materials without considering the possibility of copyright infringement.

Many new digital "publishers" are completely unaware of their potential infringement in posting texts in e-mail and in the incorporation of text, graphics, sound, and video on the World Wide Web. Both the functions of the software that support digital communication and the common paradigm of sharing in the Internet community encourage "free use" of digital texts rather than fair use.

The overwhelming response of legal analysts who follow the protectionist paradigm in interpreting the copyright law has been of extreme fear of a user's ability to copy and transmit digitized works with ease. This fear is reflected in the argument that when users make the fair use claim while assuming that individuals' creation of single copies will not harm the copyright holder, they rely too heavily on an interpretation of what users, not authors, consider reasonable. Protectionists argue that the result is minimal protection of authors' rights (Bush 72). Protectionists further argue that in light of the use of technology that allows quick and simple copying and transmission, the statutory protection is not enough. They also fear that unlicensed copying and distribution of protected work are too difficult to police (Clapes 135) and that copyright holders will suffer economic harm as a result. Lukac states that "the copyright problem is a typical one of economic threat being brought about by changing technology" (9). When intellectual products are transferred through bits instead of atoms, the only way to really protect information from widespread copying is to use encryption. But effective encryption that works well and cannot be penetrated is far from being perfected.

To some extent, authors' and publishers' fear that protection of their work will be diluted with the use of digital communication is justified, since it is a fairly common belief among users that any material that *can* be copied is available to be copied:

> To the extent that law and established social practice exists in this area, they are already in dangerous disagreement. The laws regarding unlicensed reproduction of commercial software are clear and stern . . . and rarely observed. Software piracy laws are so practically unenforceable and breaking them has become so socially acceptable that only a thin minority appears compelled, either by fear or conscience, to obey them. (Barlow)

But the response of protectionists, justifiable as it may seem, has been to work toward overtightening the interpretation of intellectual property law against fair use in an attempt to ensure protection of copyright holders' economic interests. The result is to emphasize copyright holders' financial goals rather than the policy behind the statute, to promote the creation of knowledge in society. The goal of the copyright provision is clear:

> All Americans need to realize that the copyright law is the infrastruc-
> ture supporting the program of learning in our free society—and that
> if it is to save its crucial function, the law must take into account
> not only its rewards for creators and disseminators but also reason-
> able rights for the users who provide those rewards. (Patterson and
> Lindberg 17)

Despite the provision of a statute that supports learning, as protectionists argue, authors do need legal protection of their work in order to
create incentives to continue. But the new technology produces problems in determining the source of original work in a way that was not
possible prior to digitized communication.

Esther Dyson, Brad Cox, and John Perry Barlow have suggested that
we take a new look at the economic system that rewards authors for
their work. Very few would deny that authors should reap the benefits
of their work, but these proponents of public access stance in copyright
suggest an alternate system of rewards that is more appropriate to a
world of digital information. They suggest that rather than publishers
paying authors for the right to control the copying and dissemination
of their work, the Internet could be adapted to allow for a system in
which each author's work, published on-line, could be accessed for two
or three cents per "hit" (per electronic access to the site), which would
be paid for by readers who access the material. Cox argues that authors
could reap higher economic benefit through this system than in the current system in which they must transfer their rights to publishers. This
proposed system is actually more consistent with the intent of the copyright statute in that it would ensure that authors retain rights in their work
instead of being forced to transfer those rights to publishers in order to
benefit economically. Although such a system would virtually eliminate
the role of publisher as it now exists, publishers could adapt by taking
on roles as clearinghouses for the vast amount of information that is
available on-line. Even though this proposed system is responsive to the
special character of Web publication, there are detriments as well. In roles
as clearinghouses, publishers would still maintain power to decide for
users what and what not to access. They would also, by necessity, be
divided on whether to print hard copy or digitized versions of works. If
they chose to produce important works only for Web publication, then
less technologically adept groups in society would be effectively prohibited from access, leading to the same kinds of problems with egalitarian
representation that we face with restrictive application of intellectual
property law. As the character of information changes, it is helpful to
continue thinking about how we might adapt to new economies.

Society is in the process of shifting from an industrial base to an information base, and information rather than money will become a bar-

gaining tool in economic markets (Toffler). International sources of power were formerly found in a country's natural resources, such as oil products, but today information has become the most treasured commodity. The result is that a nation's power comes from its ability to contain information. The global reach of the Internet, however, is making such containment less possible. For example, the government of the former Soviet Union attempted to keep the Chernobyl nuclear disaster secret, but unfortunately for the former Soviet leaders, the technology of satellite and Internet communication made it impossible to contain the truth, and soon every government on earth knew of the incident (Wriston 59–61).

Rather than reacting in fear of our new ability to copy and disseminate ideas quickly, we should welcome the shift that is occurring in regard to how we treat ideas and realize that our system of valuing information will have to change. Our system of economy is changing to the extent that we value the ideas in intellectual property more than the physical conveyance of those ideas. This distinction is significant in light of the 1976 Copyright Act, which severs protection of the "expression" of an idea, the conveyance, from the idea itself. Ideas are not protected under copyright, and in the new technological system of information transfer, the physical form of conveyance becomes immaterial; thus, the whole economy surrounding the transfer of information changes. "Since it is now possible to convey ideas from one mind to another without ever making them physical, we are now claiming to own ideas themselves and not merely their expression" (Barlow). This claim to the right to control information violates the constitutional basis of the statute. Even the suggestion of an Internet-based system in which the author is paid directly for work remains a problem because the conflation of ideas and expression can create a lack of accessibility to the ideas. "There is a fundamental problem with a system that requires, through technology, payment for every access to a particular expression. It defeats the original Jeffersonian purpose of seeing that ideas were available to everyone regardless of their economic station" (Barlow).

John Perry Barlow suggests a new economy altogether, in which we assign value to information on the basis of its meaningfulness and, from time to time, its scarcity. New ways to be paid for ideas could be in real-time performance and service models in which authors would be available on-line to answer questions and guide information seekers by providing ideas that would help users synthesize the material they have found. This system places more value on the ideas than the form of expression of ideas. It also places value on the ability to make meaningful connections with other people who are dealing with similar intellectual interests.

This change in the valuation of information is important, particularly for educators who are preparing students to enter the workforce and helping them to learn to analyze and assimilate into a professional community in which digital technology is paramount for communication. Students' ability to communicate effectively with text, visual layout, graphics, sound, and video is their key to accessing the social and political processes from which our American ideology arises. In order to participate in an economy of ideas (in the national conversation of participatory democracy), in which digital technology conflates ideas and their conveyance, students and other producers must be able to create the mental conveyances that contain their ideas in order to be able to communicate.

Beyond the need to convey an idea effectively, creators must also learn how to synthesize and develop new insights from the massive amount of information that is available on-line. Today our problem is not in the ability to gain access to ideas but to distinguish the worth of the material accessed. In the past, the worth of property in the form of atoms or bits was dependent on the economic framework of supply and demand. The elimination of scarcity from an economic structure necessarily changes our consideration of the valuation of information. Economic (but not necessarily monetary) power comes not from the ability to extend the quantity or range of information available but from the ability to synthesize information and make meaning of it. Negroponte asks what we would choose to transfer when we have the capability to transfer any information that exists. The implication is that access to millions of gigabytes of information is useless if its value is limited and if we lack the ability to use it.

The result of a change in economic value is to focus not on the package of the intellectual product but on the development of human thought itself. "The human mind . . . is replacing sunlight and mineral deposits as a principal new source of wealth" (Barlow). The result for copyright is that the law as it is today is inadequate to "protect" the intellectual products of creators. But the communal ideology of the Web encourages users to share information in order to jointly move toward a better future in which all in the community are able to contribute to the dialogic process of finding solutions to new problems. The Internet community, as described by Rheingold, Rushkoff, and Brand, allows for a dialogic process in which dissonance occurs within forums for working out real-life issues.

It is in the ability to connect with others in order to share information and develop thought that the power of knowledge implementation lies. Many individuals have experienced the ease and comfort of the ability to post pertinent questions and comments on e-mail news lists and receive near-immediate responses that incite new thought. Stewart Brand, Howard Rheingold, and others who describe the culture of the Internet tell of their experiences with meaningful and advantageous personal connections in the "Well" and other popular chat rooms. Many professionals know the value of "networking" for making use of inside information and personal connection to plan business moves. In addition, synthesis of information necessary for deep consideration of societal problems requires access both to individuals and to the texts that represent their thoughts. An economy of ideas that depends on synthesizing knowledge places great value on the ability to access information. Ironically, the effect of digitization of information in conflating ideas and their expression emphasizes the importance of access to ideas as well as the form in which they are conveyed.

The Challenge

Understanding the distinctions between law and policy is necessary for analyzing intellectual property law's effect on the intellectual development of our nation. Legal issues arise from conflict between individuals; the mechanism of the law attempts to provide a means to dispense with individual conflicts in a consistent, rational manner. Policy considerations, on the other hand, arise not from *individual* conflicts but from the need to ensure that the effects of law on our cultural development as a society and a nation are advantageous to our national goals. The public at large rather than the individual is the interested party in treatment of policy issues.

While the greatest basis of legal conflict is that between authors' and users' rights, the most important policy issue is treated specifically in the Constitution's intellectual property provision. The most persuasive construction of the act's statutory purpose is put forth by L. Ray Patterson and Stanley Lindberg in *The Nature of Copyright*. Patterson and Lindberg explain that the goal of the copyright act is to ensure free speech and the advancement of knowledge through our constitutional protection of the right to disseminate information. As I noted earlier, the original constitutional provisions indicate the intent to ensure the development of knowledge in society based in a congressional grant to authors of a limited monopoly of rights in their works:

> The Congress shall have the power . . . to Promote the Progress of Science and the useful Arts, by securing for limited Times to Authors and Inventors the exclusive Right to their respective Writings and Discoveries. (US Const, art. 1, sec. 8, cl. 8)

The primary goal of the provision is to ensure that intellectual products remain in the public domain in order to promote learning. To meet this goal, the law serves a regulatory function by enabling authors limited exclusive benefit of their work, subject to time and fair use limitations. Conflict over copyright results from disparate arguments: on the one hand, some legal scholars argue that the statute supports protection of authors' rights over users' rights, and on the other hand, other legal scholars note that the provision emphasizes users' rights, with both arguments made on the basis of the promotion of learning. But authors' rights are explicitly limited by the 1976 Copyright Act in order to preserve uses such as those for individual learning, criticism, and classroom educational purposes.

Although disagreement among legal experts over the real purpose behind the copyright statute continues, and the effects of digitization of information complicate arguments further, the 1976 Copyright Act includes language that would accommodate changes in technology, including television, photocopying, and computers. This new statute protects a work's expression and not the ideas by severing the content of the intellectual product from its form. In early copyright law, before the printing press was developed and used, intellectual property in the form of a single book or a sheet of music was treated much like physical property such as a cow or bale of hay. Ownership entailed exclusive physical possession over the property, and transfer of rights in the property was a transfer of the property itself. In severing the rights to the ideas of a work from the expression of the work, Congress acknowledged the change in our cultural understanding of intellectual property resultant from technological progress; intellectual products would now be treated not as physical property but as intangible entities. This change in characterization of property sent a significant message that the support of learning is the statute's primary goal.

By way of the 1976 Act, Congress also expanded the realm of the public domain and created an electronic copyright that protects work that is performed in addition to that which is published, but the most important change is embodied in section 107 of the 1976 act, which codified the judicial law in the fair use doctrine. The fair use provision makes clear that the primary goal of the statute is to promote learning. These changes notwithstanding, the conflict between authors' rights and the goal to promote knowledge, central to the copyright debate since its inception, continues.

Unfortunately, the public policy issue is often ignored in deference to concerns over economic interests. The day-to-day application of law necessarily focuses on treating conflict between individuals. Lawyers are trained specifically to meet the needs of the legal system and are economically supported by their work in this area. But the policy issues behind the statute are actually most important to us as educators and to our society as a whole because those who control the development of knowledge in a culture ultimately determine who we are as a people.

Ideology and the goals that accompany it drive our view of policy issues. Ideology determines how we view authorship, ownership, and property and ultimately affects not only how intellectual property law is controlled but how information and communication that are central to the dialogic processes within the nation are controlled, as well as determining who controls them. An examination of ideological choices in application to intellectual property thus renders important understanding of the potential effect of the law on our cultural future.

The dominant ideologies in the Internet and academic humanist communities are based on the epistemology of social construction. The body of knowledge that constructs our society is multiply authored and multiply owned, and that knowledge has been and continues to be rewritten by societal and environmental influences. The Internet and academic humanist communities encourage egalitarian access to knowledge, collaborative learning, and information sharing. The constructionist ideology calls into question whether absolute individual authorship and, thus, ownership, of knowledge are desirable or even possible.

Digitized communication also influences our understanding of authorship and ownership, as technology has done since the early history of intellectual property law. Before the printing press was invented, intellectual property was viewed as a tangible entity. Producing a book, for instance, required painstaking inscription of letters with crude inks and writing utensils. Because it was very difficult and time-consuming to create a copy, it was common to conflate the intellectual product with the tangible property of the book itself. After the development and use of the printing press, reproducing intellectual property became much simpler; thus, it was possible to sell a tangible form of intellectual expression and retain it simultaneously. Publishers often held the rights to intellectual products, since they also maintained the capability for reproduction of the work.

Our own 1976 Copyright Act reflects the change in treatment of intellectual property in its severance of protection of the expression of a work from protection of the idea in it. But today the digitization of text is affecting characterization of intellectual property even more profoundly than before. The digital "container" is itself relatively ephemeral, and although the expression of a work can still remain protected, the digital container simplifies violation of copyright because it changes the otherwise tangible form in which the intellectual property exists.

In addition, educators' and the general publics' rapid assimilation into the Internet community through the use of e-mail and the World Wide Web has further influenced views of ownership. The character of digital works makes it difficult to attach ownership, since these works are continually transformed by contributions from multiple writer/readers. In addition, the activities inherent in communication in e-mail and in the World Wide Web encourage intermingling of creators' works. The technology provides communicators with the ability to quickly and easily copy and paste materials for comment, to forward another individual's e-mail, and to link materials and copy HTML source code and graphics on the Web. The dominant ideological paradigm has been that digital communication is meant to be shared and that the goals of interaction and intellectual interchange far outweigh any concern over maintaining ownership of "individually" authored materials. This view supports the concept that knowledge is multiply owned, questions whether any work can possibly be generated by a sole author, and raises doubt that any work can or should be exclusively owned and, thus, exclusively controlled.

As a result of digital technology, the means of transferring ideas has changed. Ideas that were once contained in a tangible form of expression are now a part of an intangible one. Information that was once made of atoms can now exist in the form of bits (Negroponte 3–4) and digitization of information has caused havoc in the interpretation of the intellectual property statute. Authors' work can be copied and transferred easily, quickly, and *in toto,* and many fear economic loss as a result. Corporate entities now entering the Internet arena for the first time bring with them the protectionist values developed in the business community and fear the conventions that support free copying and dissemination of information on the World Wide Web. The result of this fear has been a backlash against the right of access to information and against the policy behind the constitutional provisions intended to ensure the advancement of knowledge.

The digitization of information creates urgency in treating intellectual property issues because it makes copying and information transfer quick and easy, encourages the commingling of authorship, creates a paradigm of free copying and dissemination of knowledge, and allows greater participatory democracy. The result is a significant change in the concept of authorship.

The dominant ideology of the legal community stands in stark contrast to that of communities that support a constructionist ideology. The dominant ideology of the law is based in the foundational, Romantic concept of authorship and, thus, ownership (Jaszi, "Toward a Theory of Copyright"), which supports the view that a single author can create, own, and control the knowledge that constructs society. In addition, although the 1976 Copyright Act explicitly severs protection of expression from that of ideas, courts commonly apply the common law to intellectual property issues on the basis of a justification derived from the "sweat of the brow" argument that authors should retain the right to work created by their own efforts. Using the common law has the effect of refocusing attention on the tangibility of the container of intellectual property, which in turn recreates an exclusive nature of ownership in intellectual products.

When courts apply this dominant legal ideology they create two types of owners of knowledge in society: those placed in privileged and politically powerful positions in society by way of their status as creators or authors of a dominant literary canon, and those who have access to money and power to acquire control and exclusive right of access to intellectual property.

The nature of law requires that it maintain at least a facade of stability in a foundational concept in order to provide consistency and order to a chaotic society. But even though few individuals in the legal community recognize it, laws are also socially constructed, usually in politically influenced contexts. The very concept of participatory democracy is based on the expectation that differing political forces will hammer out their conflicts through a national dialogic process. To inhibit access to that process is tantamount to a denial of citizenship and, as the title of this book indicates, an exercise of control over society's less powerful voices. At its base, the development of intellectual property law from a Romantic view of authorship and ownership hinders the constitutional intent of the intellectual property provision and prohibits access of minority voices to the dialogic processes of participatory democracy in the development of socially constructed laws.

Developing new law that addresses inequities seems a viable means for correcting the imbalance between legal and policy issues; however, even though our nation creates and redefines law through two separate processes, at present the policy issues behind the constitutional intellectual property provision are often ignored. The courts create law by applying precedent through the treatment of legal issues in case dispensation, and Congress creates law through the legislative process.

Case litigation, of necessity, is based on legal rather than policy issues. Case law focuses on individual factual disputes, whereas policy issues are rarely the subject of scrutiny in litigation. In fact, except in few special circumstances, lawyers who might become mired in discussions of policy would certainly do disservice to their clients. The fact is that policy issues are separate from the legal issues treated in case dispensation. A wronged party cannot bring suit on the basis of policy but must instead have legal grounding for making a claim. The result is that issues of public access to knowledge are rarely treated in the development of case law.

The legislative process, on the other hand, is the appropriate venue for policy discussion; it provides a forum for examining the broader societal impact of the developing law. However, although public policy is the focus of the legislative process, legislators with interests in intellectual property are most often lawyers who have been trained in the legal system and maintain a foundational, Romantic view of authorship, ownership, and property; their legal training in intellectual property is based in argument of legal issues regarding copyright holders' and users' rights rather than in the treatment of public policy issues concerning the publics' right of access. Public policy issues are often not evenly considered even in legislative venues. The National Information Infrastructure's (NII) White Paper, for example, was developed under the guidance of Bruce Lehman, a copyright industry lobbyist who has spent his career representing and lobbying for corporate commercial interests; these interests, of course, are almost purely economic. The many attempts lately to strengthen protectionist interests in copyright by passing restrictive intellectual property legislation (NET Act, Sonny Bono Copyright Extension Act) are a result of large corporate entities using their economic strength to take advantage of an imbalance of representation in the battle over copyright concerns regarding the Internet. Lawyers who represent corporate interests are aware of the policy goals behind the intellectual property statute and may even have some concern about the rights and needs of the average citizen, but the bottom line is that these powerful lobbying forces are well-paid representatives of parties whose only interest is economic. Very rarely, judges do consider policy issues in deciding case law, but more usual representatives of the public's noneconomic interests in intellectual property are organizations such as the American Library Association, the Digital Future Coalition, and the Electronic Frontier Foundation. Although some of their members are lawyers, few (if any) practice intellectual property law. Although these groups have submitted views to the White Paper's Working Group, and even though our adversary system of representation of conflicting interests is intended to ensure dissensus in order to reach a fairly negotiated consensus, their representative voice is weaker than that of the corporate, commercial lobbyists who have influenced development of protectionist law.

The weak and underrepresented party to this "adversary process" is the individual American citizen who has no counsel, no money, and no large lobbying body. Organizations such as the Digital Future Coalition, the Electronic Frontier Foundation, and the American Library Association struggle valiantly to combat corporate interests' advances through their demands for extreme protection of authors' rights, but these relatively small organizations have little economic support; thus, their impact is comparatively weak. The real representatives for the interests of the average citizen are educators and librarians; as educators, we bear the responsibility for fighting to protect the interests of all citizens in the right (need) to access information and to be a part of the process of creating knowledge. Those who control knowledge control what we are as a people; thus, it is of grave importance that egalitarian access be maintained in order to give *all* people a chance to participate in influencing what we are as a nation and to contribute to the dialogic process that produces the voices that control our national culture.

Society can support participatory democracy by ensuring that information be made available to all individuals regardless of political influence, economic power, or ability to create. Access allows for free speech and freedom to participate in the polylogue of the community in order to participate in recreating society as well. There is no idea that is not capable of improving knowledge (Feyerabend 47); thus, it is also advantageous to society to make information accessible to all to allow broad participation in creating that knowledge. But when dealing with protectionist-oriented corporate entities, we must rely on more than enthusiasm for the potential of an idyllic cyberspace to support knowledge creation.

The need for balanced discussion of the intellectual property issues that affect our cultural future is great. Educators must participate in the national discussion of these issues to help create a balance between legal and policy issues, as well as authors' and users' rights. Educators have a special interest in defending the constitutional intent to preserve the public's right to access information in order to support the advancement of learning. Not unlike creative writers, lawyers, doctors, and other professionals, we are both creators and users of communicative materials; we author "original" works, a basis of the grant of tenure and promotions, and we use others' "original" works in those creations. As authors, we support protection of our work from infringement by others and the right to procure economic benefit from them; as users, we need access to others' works. But our position as educators places us in a unique position in two ways: (1) our use of originally authored materials as a basis of our work in teaching falls under the provisions for educational fair use, and most important, (2) as educators we are by necessity placed into a position of responsibility for protecting the public's right of access to knowledge in support of First Amendment goals of free speech and dissemination of information. The fair use provisions are the subject of immense argument in the debate over how to balance the rights of authors against the public's need to access materials to make learning possible. But the basis of the fair use exceptions is in the message to the public that Congress supports access to information in order to encourage learning; the inclusion of fair use in the 1976 copyright statute points to the importance of this goal.

The current imbalance in favor of authors' rights makes educators likely advocates for the public's interest in access. First, as educators, our central goal is to advance learning. Second, our dominant ideology of social construction supports the public's right of access to information. Third, our positions as academics provide a means for thoughtful consideration of issues regarding the consequences of limited public access to knowledge. We support dual goals to help students participate in developing new thought and to provide egalitarian access to the knowledge-making process. *All* individuals from their distinct and diverse communities should have access to the knowledge that forms the very basis of society because access to knowledge and to the process of creating it is the first step in accessing the process of participatory democracy. Finally, educators can play important roles as public access advocates because we are a large enough group, when joined, to have an impact on the development of law. It is vital that we maintain the intended policy of the copyright statute:

> [W]hen the primary articles of commerce in a society look so much like speech as to be indistinguishable from it, and when the traditional methods of protecting their ownership have become ineffectual, attempting to fix the problem with broader and more vigorous enforcement will inevitably threaten freedom of speech. The greatest constraint on your future liberties may come not from government but from corporate legal departments laboring to protect by force what can no longer be protected by practical efficiency or general social consent. Furthermore, when Jefferson and his fellow creatures of the Enlightenment designed the system that became American copyright law, their primary objective was assuring the widespread distribution of thought, not profit. (Barlow)

Not only did the framers of the Constitution support the guarantee of freedom of speech by creating the intellectual property statute, they also ensured that all citizens would have access to learning in order to become effective participants in the democratic process.

We can examine the theoretical issues surrounding discussion of intellectual property to apply ideology in the form of pragmatic action. The first step in affecting the future begins with education concerning the issues, which can be carried out in several ways. Interested participants can become involved in discussions concerning current intellectual property issues by joining the CCCC's intellectual property e-mail discussion list, CCCC-IP.[1] Members of the CCCC may also attend the Intellectual Property Caucus, which is consistently scheduled during the first day of the CCCC annual conference. Participants not only hear presentations on pertinent issues and news regarding the most current developments in the law, but they are asked to participate in group discussions of the issues to determine actions that the CCCC organization may want to take in the future. Active members with special interests in intellectual property issues may also be asked to serve on committees or task forces to work closely with issues that affect future representation of CCCC regarding intellectual property issues.

In addition to education, a number of other actions can be taken that can ultimately have a great impact on the development and application of intellectual property law. We can work individually to lobby political representatives by writing letters and e-mail posts that represent views on pending legislation. Educators can also make issues regarding intellectual property, the ramifications of use and misuse, and plagiarism a subject in their classes so that students begin to examine the impact of the law on their work and for their futures. Perhaps most important, academicians should make fearless use of materials, as encouraged by the fair use provision for educational uses of copyrighted work. When consistent and reasonable use of copyrighted materials becomes common practice among academicians, interpretations of the intellectual property law will be shaped in ways that are favorable to egalitarian access to information. Alternately, a fearful response to warnings against all use of copyrighted material can have a chilling effect on the development of knowledge, thwarting the constitutional intent of the statute.

The actions possible within this framework of guidance can be broad, and each individual must make the final decision regarding the uses he or she will make. The guidelines for fair use are available in detail in chapter 3, but it may be helpful to reiterate them here. Legality of action is determined constructively, on a case-by-case basis, and the fair use guidelines are applied in connection to one another. Adjudicators examine the use of copyrighted materials as an aggregate of characterizations; thus, no one of the characterizations provided in the guidelines would be sufficient to make a determination of fair use.

Following the guidelines, however, I summarize the concepts separately. First, if the purpose and character of use indicates absence of intent to gain economic benefit from the use, the fair use defense can be supported. The nature of the copyrighted work also plays a role in a court's determination of fair use; thus, if the use is educational and nonprofit in nature, provides important criticism of government action, or reports a newsworthy event, the likelihood of support of the fair use defense increases. A defense of fair use is often supported when an insubstantial amount of a work is used for a limited period of time. In addition, absence of economic harm to the copyright holder usually provides a general principle of guidance in support of fair use of materials that may be questionable.

Difficulties arise when untested uses of materials are made, which is the case when instructors use the Internet as a basis for distributing classroom materials. For instance, an instructor of a distance learning class, under time constraints and after fruitless attempts to locate the copyright holder of a particularly pertinent source of material, wishes to upload a short piece of text into a World Wide Web page for students to use for classroom purposes. If she loads it to a location on the Web but does not create links that would enable viewers other than her students to access the file, the likelihood that the use would be protected under the fair use exceptions is relatively high. If she links it to a file that is easily accessible by users other than her students, her defense loses strength because the character of the use is no longer limited strictly to educational purposes *within* her classroom. But if the need for the content of the document is great, the instructor might balance that need against potential for infringement and decide to use the copy even in light of the possibility of infringement. In a very different situation, in which her purpose is to create an educational site that includes copyrighted work and charge a per-hit fee for browsers around the world, the instructor's likelihood of effective use of the fair use defense is low.

A typical situation arises when students copy graphic images to incorporate into their web pages created for class projects. If the purpose of their copying is only to ornament pages, the likelihood that a court will uphold the fair use defense would be low. If students create pages with the intention of advertising for the companies for which they work, the use is even less likely to be considered fair. However, if students make critical comments regarding the design or content of graphics, the strength of their defense increases. If the criticism brings new knowledge to light concerning a powerful private entity or government office, the use is even more likely to be fair. Students and instructors can make judgments about their uses, in part, by balancing the need against the possibility of infringement. If the need is great and the risk of infringement is low, the decision should be clear. The difficulty in making decisions rises when the balance is close.

But students and instructors who copy materials for nonprofit, educational purposes have almost nothing to fear from potential threat of suit. Their use is most often insubstantial and not worthy of the time, effort, and cost that a plaintiff would have to invest to pursue an unlikely victory. Even when plaintiffs are likely to win in court, their first remedy before filing suit is to enjoin the infringer from using the protected material. This is most often accomplished by sending a letter of notification of the violation, to which the offender responds by discontinuing the potentially illegal use. Usually it is when a plaintiff has been harmed economically that litigation is reasonable and worth pursuing.

There are, however, strong advocates of a protectionist stance toward use of copyrighted materials; they often go beyond the boundaries of reason. Strict interpretation of the NII White Paper, currently under congressional debate for enactment into law, makes possible the argument that it is a copyright violation simply to click on a link in order to upload material from a site for viewing. By the same token, proponents of a strong protectionist view also argue that providing a link on a home page to a site at another location is itself a violation of copyright restrictions. These arguments are, of course, extreme because following these strict limitations would make the whole system of the Web ineffectual; its very existence depends not only on the ability but the desire of Web participants to link materials to create interconnection among sites.

Although the law allows for the possibility of suits on these bases, the likelihood of this kind of frivolous legal action is low. Most educators can make good faith use of materials for educational, class-related purposes without fear of suit. Educators should use materials that are necessary for teaching to their best ability. Their good faith use of materials should push them to use the fair use exceptions as they were intended; to ensure the advancement of learning.

Although the law must be pushed to its limits to ensure that our future access to information is protected, it is also important that educators develop ethical standards for using materials; we can create extralegal, self-imposed limitations on use that could harm creators or publishers. Of necessity, we must push to maintain maximum access within the range that the law allows because, once imposed, law provides little leeway for change within the confines of precedential interpretation and because that law is slow to change through the legislative process. As a community, we should begin to develop standards for use that take into consideration our multiple and changing needs as educators, creators, and users of protected materials.

Probably the most important impact that educators can make for ensuring that the law remain flexible enough to allow egalitarian access to the knowledge base in society is to work as members of large and politically visible organizations such as CCCC, NCTE, ATTW, and MLA. Participants should also urge these academic organizations to develop guidelines for using educational materials and encourage such organizations to create forces to lobby Congress in favor of educators' goals.

By virtue of our status as educators, we may be the only group who can bring intellectual property issues to light in a balanced manner, not only for students but for the public at large. Gaining an understanding of intellectual property issues is central to understanding our rights as users and producers of knowledge. The actions we take to influence egalitarian access to information can have long-term ramifications for society, because authorship generates control, control generates authority, and authority generates power. We should take every step necessary to ensure that the controlling voices of the few but powerful are balanced by the yet-unheard voices of the weaker multitudes.

Notes

Works Cited

Index

Notes

Introduction

1. See also http://swissnet.ai.mit.edu/6805/readings-ip.html.

1. Protective Control for Intellectual Products

1. Refer to patent section of chapter 2 for more information.

2. Copyrights and Duties

1. Part two discusses the theoretical ramifications of the characterization of authorship in detail, while this section focuses specifically on the pragmatic application of the law in this regard.

2. See Herrington, "Who Owns My Work?" and "Work for Hire" for more detailed treatment of U.S. work for hire issues.

3. Fair Use, Access, and Cultural Construction

1. See *Rosemont Enterprises, Inc. v. Random House, Inc.* 366 F.2d 303, 307 (2d Cir. 1966) and *Consumers Union of the United States, Inc. v. General Signal Corp.* 730 F.2d 47 (2d Cir. 1984).

2. See *Sony Corporation of America v. Universal City Studios, Inc.* 104 S. Ct. 774, 220 U.S.P.Q. 655 (1984).

3. See Bond, Echerou, and Wassom for more.

4. See figures 1 and 2 and see also Warnick for more on website parodies.

5. The District Court decision in *Acuff-Rose Music Inc. v. Campbell* is reported at 754 F. Supp. 1150 (M.D. Tenn. 1991); Oscar Brand's statement is quoted in the Circuit Court opinion at 972 F.2d 1429, 1433 (6th Cir. 1992). The Court of Appeals decision in the 2 Live Crew case, *Acuff-Rose, Inc. v. Campbell,* is reported at 972 F.2d 1492 (6th Cir. 1992), and the Supreme Court decision, *Campbell v. Acuff-Rose,* at 510 U.S. 569, 127 L.Ed.2d 500, 524.

6. See Herrington, "Interdependency of Fair Use and the First Amendment" for more detail.

7. See *Harper & Row, Publishers, Inc. v. Nation Enterprizes,* 723 F.2d. 195 (2d Cir. 1983) and *Consumers Union of the United States, Inc. v. General Signal Corp.,* 724 F.2d 104 (2d Cir. 1983).

4. Law and Policy: The Balance in Cyberspace

1. See Bush, Clapes.

2. Send e-mail to listproc-request@counsel.com with the message "subscribe cyberspace-law (your first name and your last name)."

5. Controlling Construction: The Internet, Law, and Humanistic Studies

1. Among numerous sources treating Internet community and cultural issues are Jones, Kiesler, Smith and Kollack, Moore, and Loader.

2. See Ronald Dworkin's *Law's Empire* for extensive explanation.

6. Controlling Ideologies: The Internet, Law, and Humanistic Studies

1. See Kleinman for an enlightening treatment of the history of the concept of "property" in intellectual property.

2. In the long oral tradition of folk tunes and tales, it was difficult to pinpoint ownership of works that were a part of this body; thus, these items rarely fell into the category of adjudicated intellectual property.

7. The New Millennium and Controlling Voices

1. Information for how to join, in addition to other pertinent intellectual property information, is located on the CCCC-IP web site at http://www.ncte.org/cccc-ip/welcome.html.

Works Cited

Acuff-Rose Music Inc. v. Campbell. 972 F.2d 1492. 6th Cir. 1992.

"Adbusters: Spoof Ads."(http://adbusters.org/spoofads/fashion/escape/) 4 Apr. 2000.

American Heritage Dictionary. 2d ed. Boston: Houghton, 1982.

Andrews, George Reid, and Herrick Chapman, eds. *The Social Construction of Democracy, 1870–1990.* New York: New York UP, 1995.

Apple Computer, Inc., v. Microsoft Corporation. U.S. Court of Appeals. 9th Cir. 1994.

Association of American University Presses. (http://aaupnet.org) 29 June 1999.

Balkin, J. M. *Cultural Software.* New Haven: Yale UP, 1998.

Barlow, John Perry. "The Economy of Ideas." (http://swissnet.ai.mit.edu/6095/articles/barlow-economy-of-ideas.html) 4 Oct. 1996.

Barrett, Edward, ed. *Sociomedia: Multimedia, Hypermedia, and the Social Construction of Knowledge.* Cambridge: MIT P, 1992.

Bazerman, Charles, and James Paradis, eds. *Textual Dynamics of the Professions.* Madison: U of Wisconsin P, 1991.

Berger, Peter L., and Thomas Luckman. *The Social Construction of Reality: A Treatise in the Sociology of Knowledge.* Garden City, NY: Doubleday, 1969.

Berkenkotter, Carol, Thomas Huckin, and John Ackerman. "Social Context and Socially Constructed Texts." Bazerman and Paradis 191–215.

Berlin, James. *Rhetoric and Reality: Writing Instruction in American Colleges, 1900–1985.* Carbondale: Southern Illinois UP, 1987.

Black, Henry Campbell. *Black's Law Dictionary.* 5th ed. St. Paul: West, 1979.

Blyler, Nancy R., and Charlotte Thralls, eds. *Professional Communication: The Social Perspective.* Newbury Park, CA: Sage, 1993.

Boiarsky, Carolyn. "The Relationship Between Cultural and Rhetorical Conventions: Engaging in International Communication." *Technical Communication Quarterly* 4 (1995): 245–60.

Bolter, Jay David. Keynote address to the Conference on College Composition and Communication Intellectual Property Caucus, Atlanta, 24 Mar. 1999.

———. *Writing Space: The Computer, Hypertext, and the History of Writing.* Hillsdale, NJ: Erlbaum, 1991.

Bond, Nicole M. "Linking and Framing on the Internet: Liability under Trademark and Copyright Law." *DePaul Business Law Journal* 11 (fall/winter 1998): 185–228.

Brand, Stewart. *The Media Lab: Inventing the Future at MIT.* New York: Penguin, 1987.

Brandt, Deborah. *Literacy as Involvement: The Acts of Writers, Readers, and Texts.* Carbondale: Southern Illinois UP, 1990.

Brinson, J. Dianne, and Mark Radcliffe. *Multimedia Law Handbook: A Practical Guide for Developers and Publishers.* Menlo Park, CA: Ladera, 1994.

Bruffee, Kenneth A. "Collaborative Learning and the Conversation of Mankind." *College English* 46 (1984): 635–52.

Bush, George P. *Technology and Copyright.* Mt. Airy, MD: Lomond Systems, 1972.

Campbell v. Acuff-Rose Music, Inc. 510 U.S. 569, 114 S. Ct. 1164. 1994.

Castle Rock Entertainment, Inc., v. Carol Publishing Group, Inc. 47 U.S.P.Q.2d 1321. 2d Cir. 1998.

Cavazos, Edward A., and Gavino Morin. *Cyberspace and the Law: Your Rights and Duties in the Online World.* Cambridge: MIT P, 1996.

Clapes, Anthony Lawrence. *Software, Copyright, and Competition: The "Look and Feel" of the Law.* New York: Quorum, 1989.

Consumers Union of the United States, Inc. v. General Signal Corp. 724 F.2d 104. 2d Cir. 1983.

Coombe, Rosemary. *The Cultural Life of Intellectual Properties: Authorship, Appropriation, and the Law.* Durham, NC: Duke UP, 1998.

———. "Objects of Property and Subjects of Politics: Intellectual Property Laws and Democratic Dialogue." Dennis Patterson.

Cox, Brad. *Superdistribution: Objects as Property on the Electronic Frontier.* (http://web.gmu.edu/bcox) 6 Oct. 1996.

Crews, Kenneth. "The *MDS* Decision and Fair Use for Coursepacks." (http://arl.cni.org/scomm/copyright/mds.crews.html.) 15 Mar. 1997.

Danow, David K. "Dialogic Perspectives: The East European View." *Russian Literature* 20 (1986): 119–42.

Dennis v. United States. 341 U.S. 494. 1951.

"Drudge Report: Monica Blows President Bill Clinton on the Presidential Seal!" (http://www.startingpage.com/html/drudge.html).

Duncan, Dan. "The Internet and Intellectual Property Rights." Cyberspace Law Institute. C-Span. 6 May 1996.

Dworkin, Ronald. *Law's Empire.* Cambridge: Harvard UP, 1986.

Dyson, Esther. "Intellectual Property on the Net." (http://www.eff.org/pub/publications/Esther_Dyson/ip-on-the-net.article).

Echerou, Ike O. "Linking to Trouble: Legal Liability Emanating from Hyperlinks on the World Wide Web." *Journal of Proprietary Rights* 10.2 (1992): 1–18.

Faigley, Lester. "Nonacademic Writing: The Social Perspective." Odell and Goswami 231–48.

Fair Use Doctrine. 17 U.S.C. sec. 107. 1978.

Feyerabend, Paul. *Against Method: Outline of an Anarchistic Theory of Knowledge.* London: Verso, 1975.

Foremski, Tom. "Multimedia Markets and Copyright Laws." *International Yearbook of Law Computers and Technology* 7 (1993): 217.

Friedman, Lawrence M. "Legal Culture and Social Development." *Law and Society Review* 4 (1969): 29–44.

Fuller, Lon. *Anatomy of the Law.* New York: Praeger, 1968.

Galler, Bernard A. *Software and Intellectual Property Protection.* Westport, CT: Quorum, 1995.

Geertz, Clifford. "Thick Description: Toward an Interpretive Theory of Culture." *The Interpretation of Cultures.* Ed. Clifford Geertz. London: Hutchinson, 1975.

———, ed. *The Interpretation of Cultures.* New York: Basic, 1977.

Glen, Frederick. *The Social Psychology of Organizations.* London: Methuen, 1975.

Grossman, Joel B., and Mary H. Grossman. *Law and Change in Modern America.* Pacific Palisades, CA: Goodyear, 1971.

Gurak, Laura J. "Technical Communication, Copyright, and the Shrinking Public Domain." *Computers and Composition* 14 (1998): 329–42.

Gusfield, Joseph. *New Social Movements from Ideology to Identity.* Philadelphia: Temple UP, 1994.

Habermas, Jürgen. "Philosophy as Stand-in and Interpreter." *After Philosophy.* Ed. Kenneth Baynes et al. Cambridge: MIT P, 1987.

———. *The Theory of Communicative Action.* Trans. Thomas McCarthy. Boston: Beacon, 1984.

———. *Toward a Rational Society.* Trans. Jeremy Shapiro. Boston: Beacon, 1968.

Hafner, Katie, and Matthew Lyon. *Where Wizards Stay Up Late.* New York: Simon, 1996.

Halley, Jeffrey A. "Bakhtin and the Sociology of Culture: Polyphony in the Interaction of Object and Audience." *Critical Studies* 1 (1989): 163–79.

Handa, Carolyn. *Computers and Community: Teaching Composition in the Twenty First Century.* Portsmouth, NH: Boynton, 1991.

Harper & Row, Publishers, Inc. v. Nation Enterprises. 723 F.2d 195. 2d Cir. 1983.

Harris, Nigel. *Beliefs in Society: The Problem of Ideology.* London: Watts, 1968.

Hawisher, Gail E., Paul LeBlanc, Charles Moran, and Cynthia L. Selfe. *Computers and the Teaching of Writing in Higher Education, 1979–1994: A History.* Norwood, NJ: Ablex, 1996.

Heim, Michael. *Electric Language: A Philosophical Study of Word Processing.* New Haven: Yale UP, 1987.

Henry, Nicholas. *Copyright: Information Technology, Public Policy.* New York: Decker, 1975.

Herrington, TyAnna K. "The Interdependency of Fair Use and the First Amendment." *Computers and Composition Special Issue: Intellectual Property* 15.2 (1998): 125–43.

———. "Who Owns My Work? The State of Work for Hire for Academics in Technical Communication." *Journal of Business and Technical Communication* 13.2 (Apr. 1999).

———. "Work for Hire for Non-academic Creators." *Journal of Business and Technical Communication* 13.4 (Oct. 1999).

Herrnstein, Richard, and Charles Murray. *The Bell Curve: Intelligence and Class Structure in American Life*. New York: Free P, 1994.

Hoebel, E. Adamson. *The Law of Primitive Man*. Cambridge: Harvard UP, 1954.

Howard, Rebecca Moore. "Plagiarisms, Authorships, and the Academic Death Penalty." *College English* 57 (1995): 788–806.

Jaszi, Peter. "On the Author Effect: Contemporary Copyright and Collective Creativity." Woodmansee and Jaszi 30–68.

———. "Toward a Theory of Copyright: The Metamorphoses of 'Authorship.'" *Duke Law Journal* (1991): 455–502.

Jones, Steven G., ed. *Virtual Culture: Identity and Communication in Cybersociety*. Thousand Oaks, CA: Sage, 1997.

Karjala, Dennis. *Opposing Copyright Extension*. (http://www.public.asu.edu/~dkarjala/).

Kiesler, Sara, ed. *Culture of the Internet*. Mahwah, NJ: Erlbaum, 1997.

Kleinman, Neil. "Don't Fence Me In: Copyright, Property, and Technology." *Readerly/Writerly Texts* (fall/winter 1995): 9–50.

Kolko, Beth E. "Intellectual Property in Synchronous and Collaborative Virtual Space." *Computers and Composition Special Issue: Intellectual Property* 15.2 (1998): 163–83.

Kuhn, Thomas. *The Structure of Scientific Revolutions*. Chicago: U of Chicago P, 1970.

Landow, George P., ed. *The Digital Word: Text-Based Computing in the Humanities*. Cambridge: MIT P, 1993.

Lanham, Richard A. *The Electronic Word: Democracy, Technology, and the Arts*. Chicago: U of Chicago P, 1993.

Latchaw, Joan S., and Jeffrey R. Galin. "Shifting Boundaries of Intellectual Property: Authors and Publishers Negotiating the WWW." *Computers and Composition Special Issue: Intellectual Property* 15.2 (1998): 145–62.

Lawrence, John Shelton. "Donald Duck v. Chilean Socialism: A Fair Use Exchange." Lawrence and Timburg 45–60.

Lawrence, John Shelton, and Bernard Timburg, eds. *Fair Use and Free Inquiry: Copyright Law and the New Media*. Newark, NJ: Ablex, 1989.

Lay, Mary M., and William M. Karis, eds. *Collaborative Writing in Industry: Investigations in Theory and Practice*. Amityville, NY: Baywood, 1991.

Lehman, Bruce A. *Intellectual Property and the National Information Infrastructure: The Report of the Working Group on Intellectual Property Rights*. Washington, D.C.: U.S. Dept. of Commerce, 1995.

Leibovitz v. Paramount Pictures Corporation. U.S.P.Q.2d 1834. 2d Cir. 1998.

Levinson, Sanford, and J. M. Balkin. "Law, Music, and Other Performing Arts." Dennis Patterson 57–118.

Lindey, Alexander. *Plagiarism and Originality*. Westport, CT: Greenwood, 1974.

Loader, Brian D., ed. *The Governance of Cyberspace: Politics, Technology and Global Restructuring*. New York: Routledge, 1997.

Lukac, George J., ed. *Copyright: The Librarian and the Law*. New Brunswick, NJ: Rutgers U Graduate School of Library Service, 1972.

Lunsford, Andrea, and Susan West. "Intellectual Property and Composition Studies." *CCC* 47 (1996): 383–411.

Minar, David H., and Scott Geer. *The Concept of Community: Readings with Interpretations*. Chicago: Aldine, 1969.

Moore, Dinty W. *The Emperor's Virtual Clothes: The Naked Truth about the Internet Culture*. Chapel Hill, NC: Algonquin, 1995.

Moulthrop, Stuart, and Nancy Kaplan. "They Become What They Behold: The Futility of Resistance in the Space of Electronic Writing." *Literacy and Computers: The Complications of Teaching and Learning With Technology (Research and Scholarship in Composition)*. Ed. Cynthia Selfe and Susan Hilligos. New York: MLA, 1994. 220–37.

Mulkay, Michael. *Science and the Sociology of Knowledge*. London: Allen, 1979.

Myers, Greg. "Stories and Styles in Two Molecular Biology Review Articles." Bazerman and Paradis 45–75.

Negroponte, Nicholas. *Being Digital*. New York: Knopf, 1995.

Neitzke, Frederic William. *A Software Law Primer*. New York: Van Nostrand, 1984.

Nielsen, Kai. "Skeptical Remarks on the Scope of Philosophy: Rorty v. Habermas." *Social Theory and Practice* 19 (1993): 117–60.

1976 Copyright Act. 17 U.S.C. 1982.

Nisbet, Robert A. *Community and Power*. New York: Oxford UP, 1962.

No Electronic Theft Act. H.R. 2256. Dec. 1997.

Ocampo, Raymond L., and David S. Shellenhase. "The Multimedia Market-place: A Proposal for Handling Rights in the Digital Age." *California Lawyer* 14 (1994): 70–72.

Odell, Lee, and Dixie Goswami, eds. *Writing in Nonacademic Settings*. New York: Guilford, 1985.

Olafsen, F. "Habermas as a Philosopher." *Ethics* (1990): 641–57.

The Onion. (http://www.theonion.com/onion3610/infograph_3610.html) 4 Apr. 2000.

Patry, William F. *The Fair Use Privilege in Copyright Law*. Washington, D.C.: Bureau of National Affairs, 1995.

Patterson, Dennis, ed. *Postmodernism and Law*. New York: New York UP, 1994.

Patterson, L. Ray. "Private Copyright and Public Communication: Free Speech Endangered." *Vanderbilt Law Review* 28 (1975): 1161–211.

Patterson, L. Ray, and Stanley W. Lindberg. *The Nature of Copyright*. Athens: U of Georgia P, 1991.

Plant, Raymond. *Community and Ideology: An Essay in Applied Social Philosophy*. London: Routledge, 1974.

Porter, James. "The Role of Law, Policy, and Ethics in Corporate Composing: Toward a Practical Ethics for Professional Writing." Blyler and Thralls 128–43.

Post, David. *The Internet and Intellectual Property Rights*. Cyberspace Law Institute. C-Span. 6 May 1996.

Princeton University Press v. Michigan Document Services, Inc. (http:// www.kentlaw.edu/cgi-bin/ldn_news/-T+law.listserv.cni-copyright) 5 Oct. 1996.

Publications Int'l Ltd. v. Bally Mfg. Corp. 215 U.S.P.Q. 861. 1982.

Quinto v. Legal Times of Washington, Inc. 506 F. Supp. 560. 1981.

Rheingold, Howard. *The Virtual Community: Finding Connection in a Computerized World.* London: Secker, 1994.

Rose, Lance. *Netlaw: Your Rights in the Online World.* Berkeley, CA: Osborne, 1995.

Rosemont Enterprises, Inc. v. Random House, Inc. 366 F.2d 307. 2d Cir. 1966.

Rosenfield, Harry N. "The American Constitution, Free Inquiry, and the Law." Lawrence and Timburg 281–304.

Rubin v. Boston Magazine Co. 645 F.2d 84. 1st Cir. 1981.

Rude, Carolyn. "Managing Publications According to Legal and Ethical Standards." *Publications Management Essays for Technical Communication.* Ed. O. Jane Allen and Lynn H. Deming. Amityville, NY: Baywood, 1994.

Rushkoff, Douglas. *Cyberia: Life in the Trenches of Hyperspace.* San Francisco: Harper, 1994.

Salinger, J. D. *Catcher in the Rye.* New York: Little, 1991.

Salinger v. Random House, Inc. 811 F.2d 90. U.S. Ct. of Appeals, 2d Cir. 1987.

Samuelson, Pamela. "Digital Media and the Changing Face of Intellectual Property Law." *Rutgers Computer and Technology Law Journal* 16 (1990): 323–40.

———. *Legally Speaking: The NII Intellectual Property Report.* (http:// www.eff.org/pub/Intellectual_property/nii_ip_report.article) 5 Oct. 1996.

San Juan, E., Jr. "From Bakhtin to Gramsci: Intertextuality, Praxis, Hegemony." *New Orleans Review* 18 (1990): 75–85.

Shevstova, Maria. "Dialogism in the Novel and Bakhtin's Theory of Culture." *New Literary History* 23 (1992): 747–63.

Simon, David F. *Computer Law Handbook: Software Protection, Contracts, Litigation, Forms.* Philadelphia: American Law Institute–American Bar Association Committee on Continuing Professional Education, 1990.

Smith, Marc, and Peter Kollock. *Communities in Cyberspace.* New York: Routledge, 1999.

Sonny Bono Copyright Term Extension Act. S 505. Oct. 1998.

Sony Corporation of America v. Universal City Studios, Inc. 104 S. Ct. 774. 1984.

Spilka, Rachel, ed. *Writing in the Workplace: New Research Perspectives.* Carbondale: Southern Illinois UP, 1993.

Strong, William S. *The Copyright Book: A Practical Guide.* Cambridge: MIT P, 1990.

Swan, Jim. "Touching Words: Helen Keller, Plagiarism, Authorship." Woodmansee and Jaszi 57–100.

Thibault, Paul. "Narrative Discourse as a Multi-Level System of Communication: Some Theoretical Proposals Concerning Bakhtin's Dialogic Principle." *STCL* 9 (1984): 89–117.

TicketMaster Corp. v. Microsoft Corp. No. 97-3055DPP. C.D. Cal. complaint filed 28 Apr. 1997.

Toffler, Alvin. *The Third Wave.* New York: Bantam, 1991.

U.S. Constitution. Art. 1, sec. 8, cl. 8.

Wainright Securities, Inc. v. Wall Street Transcript Corp. 418 F. Supp. 620. 1976.

Warnick, Barbara. "Appearance or Reality? Political Parody on the Web in Campaign '96." *Critical Studies in Mass Communication* 15 (1998): 306–24.

Warren, M. "Can Participatory Democracy Produce Better Selves? Psychological Dimensions of Habermas's Discursive Model of Democracy." *Political Psychology* (1993): 209–34.

The Washington Post Co. v. Total News, Inc. 97 CIV 1190. S.D.N.Y. complaint filed 6 June 1997.

Wassom, Brian D. "Copyright Implications of 'Unconventional Linking' on the World Wide Web: Framing, Deep Linking, and Inlining." *Case Western Reserve Law Review* 49 (fall 1998): 181–256.

Weiss, Timothy. "Bruffee, the Bakhtin Circle, and the Concept of Collaboration." Lay and Karis 31–48.

White-Smith Music Pub. Co. v. Apollo Co. 209 U.S. 1. 1908.

Woodmansee, Martha. "On the Author Effect: Recovering Collectivity." Woodmansee and Jaszi 15–28.

Woodmansee, Martha, and Peter Jaszi. "The Law of Texts: Copyright in the Academy." *College English* 57 (1995): 769–87.

———, eds. *The Construction of Authorship: Textual Appropriation in Law and Literature.* Durham, NC: Duke UP, 1994.

Wriston, Walter B. *The Twilight of Sovereignty: How the Information Revolution Is Transforming Our World.* New York: Scribner's, 1992.

Zuboff, Shoshana. *In the Age of the Smart Machine: The Future of Work and Power.* New York: Basic, 1988.

Index

access, 5, 18, 23, 40, 59–76, 77, 78, 80, 81, 88, 100, 104–7, 120, 121, 123, 124, 125, 126, 127, 130, 131, 132, 135, 136, 140, 142, 143, 147, 149, 150
Acuff-Rose Music, Inc., 6, 7
advancement of knowledge. *See* knowledge creation
agency partnership law, 27, 45
American Association of University Presses, 17
American Library Association, 148
amount and substantiality, 59, 60, 75
Apple Computer, 48
Apple Corp. v. Microsoft, Inc., 48–49, 58
ARPANET, 93, 94
ASCAP, 37, 55, 137
authoritarian stance, 2, 10

Bakhtin, Mikhail, 104, 105, 107
balance of rights, 3, 6, 7, 8, 30, 40, 59, 121, 149
Balkin, J. M., 99
Barlow, John Perry, 137, 140, 141
Bart Simpson. *See* Simpson, Bart
"Beat Generation," 109
Beethoven, 99
Bell Curve, The (Murray and Hernstein), 5
Berger, Peter, 94
Berlin, James, 105, 112
Berne Treaty, 46
Bizzelle, Patricia, 105
BMI, 37, 55, 137

Bolter, Jay David, 118, 119
Brand, Oscar, 70
Brand, Stewart, 95, 142, 143
Bruffee, Kenneth, 94, 104

Calvin Klein Escape (advertisement), 67, 68
Campbell v. Acuff-Rose Music, Inc., 6
Castle Rock Entertainment, Inc. v. Carol Publishing Group, Inc., 70
Catcher in the Rye (Salinger), 109
CCCC, 19, 150, 151
CCCC-IP, 19, 150
CCCC-IP Caucus, 119
censorship, 126, 132, 133, 134
Census 2000, 69
Chernobyl, 141
Church of Scientology, ix
clean room defense, 35, 49, 50
Clinton, President William J., 110
CNI-IP, 116
collaboration, 9, 13, 42, 101, 104, 113, 116, 120, 127, 130, 131, 147
collections and anthologies, 73
commissioned work, 44
common law, 17, 37, 75, 78, 122, 123, 124, 125, 127, 129, 131, 146, 147
communicative action, 104–7
compilations, 74
Computers and Composition (journal), 19
Constitution, the, 3, 5, 7, 8, 15, 16, 41, 77, 81, 96, 100, 121, 124, 125, 143, 150
constitutional law, xii, 4, 27

constitutional principle, 36, 37, 40, 116, 125, 126, 149, 151
constitutional provision, 3, 7, 36, 37, 113, 121, 124, 143, 146
constructed ideologies, 11
constructionism, 7, 10
constructionist ideology, 2, 10, 127
Consumers Union of the United States, Inc. v. General Signal Corp., 71
contract law, 27, 35, 52–54
controlling law, 1, 4, 8
Coombe, Rosemary, 88, 133
copyright, 35–38
copyright control, 41–43
Copyright Extension Act. *See* Sonny Bono Copyright Extension Act
Council of European Community, 49
course pack, 12, 67
Cox, Brad, 140
critical comment, 30, 59, 61, 64, 111
criticism, 2, 61, 144
cultural construction, 59–76
Cultural Life of Intellectual Properties: Authorship, Appropriation, and the Law, The (Coombe), 88
Cyber-law list, 79, 80
cyberspace, 18, 77–83, 117, 118, 149

democracy, 104, 150
derivative work, 56, 57
dialogic process, 8, 21, 101, 102, 104–7, 114, 134, 142, 145, 147
Digital Future Coalition, 148
digital media, x, 17, 115
Digital Word, The (Landow), 118
digitization, 10, 80, 114, 117, 146
digitized communication, 78, 135, 138, 140, 145
digitized information, 12, 30, 35, 48, 57, 64, 65, 78, 81, 98, 114, 115, 118, 119, 120, 129, 130, 131, 136, 137, 139, 143, 144
Disney Corporation, 126, 134
dissensus, 98, 104, 107, 125
dissonance, 8, 9, 88, 90, 101
distance learning, 18, 21, 77, 82, 98, 152

dominant ideologies, 1, 2, 9, 22, 90, 92, 111, 113, 114, 120, 145
Dorfman, Ariel, 134
Dr. Seuss, 71
Drudge, Matt, 110
Duncan, Dan, 15
Dyson, Esther, 140

Edison, Thomas, 5
educational purpose, 59, 60, 64–67, 78
educators, xi, xii, 2, 3, 4, 8, 10, 11, 12, 13, 14, 16, 20, 27, 28, 32, 59, 60, 65, 73, 77, 79, 82, 83, 88, 92, 96, 98, 99, 113, 114, 127, 129, 142, 144, 145, 149, 150, 151, 152, 153
egalitarian access, 1, 60, 83, 104, 120, 132, 134, 135, 145, 150, 153, 154
egalitarian representation, 23, 107, 131, 136, 140
Electronic Frontier Foundation, 148
"Employee Nondisclosure Agreement," 46
exercises, 74–75

fair use, xi, xii, 7, 12, 13, 30, 38, 41, 59–76, 79, 82, 122, 124, 132, 134, 139, 144, 149, 150, 151, 152
FDA, 103
first amendment, 5, 6, 61, 62, 67, 71, 72, 73, 134, 149
fixation, 35, 38, 40, 55, 77, 78
foundational ideology, 2, 9, 121, 126, 147, 148
foundationalism, 91, 106
free press, 36
free speech, 3, 6, 67, 71, 72, 126, 132, 134, 136
"Frost King" (Keller), 54
Fuller, Lon, 61

Gates, Bill, 126
Geertz, Clifford, 89
genius, 127, 136
goodwill, 28–30
Gurak, Laura, 19

Habermas, Jürgen, 14, 106, 107

Henry, Nicholas, 36
Hernstein, Richard, 5
heteroglossia, 104, 105
Howard, Rebecca Moore, 54
How to Read Donald Duck (Dorfman and Mattelart), 134
Hubbard, L. Ron, 63
hypertext, 114, 118, 119, 135
Hypertext (Lanham), 118

ideas and expression, 47–48, 52, 54, 122, 123, 129, 141, 146
ideologies, 2, 8, 9, 23, 40, 87, 89, 91, 96, 97, 104, 105, 111, 112, 116, 118, 120, 126, 129, 130, 131, 135, 142, 144, 145, 146, 147, 150
independent contractor, 32, 45
information control, 1, 4, 8, 121
infringement, 11, 30, 35, 39, 49, 57–58, 60, 69, 72, 74, 78, 82, 124, 138, 139
international law, 46–47
Internet, 3, 8, 9, 10, 11, 13, 17, 18, 20, 21, 22, 23, 38, 39, 81, 82, 83, 87, 88, 92, 93, 94, 95, 96, 98, 104, 105, 108, 109, 110, 111, 114, 116, 118, 119, 127, 129, 130, 131, 136, 140, 141, 146
in terrorem effect, 81, 82

Jaszi, Peter, 18
joint author, 42–43
joint work, 42–43

Kairos (journal), 19
Keller, Helen, 54
knowledge control, 1, 4, 115, 120, 127, 130, 131, 135, 149
knowledge creation, 1, 2, 4, 8, 9, 10, 20, 21, 22, 59, 60, 82, 87, 91, 112, 113, 114, 121, 122, 126, 129, 130, 131, 132, 143, 145, 146, 149

Landow, George, 118, 119, 135, 136
Lanham, Richard, 118, 119, 135, 136
Lawrence, John Shelton, 134
Leibovitz, Annie, 70

Levinson, Sanford, 99
limited monopoly, 36, 40, 122
Lindberg, Stanley, 124, 143
Lindey, Alexander, 51
Lone Ranger, the, ix
Luckman, Thomas, 94
Lunsford, Andrea, 18

Macintosh, 58
market value, 60, 75–76
Mattelart, Armand, 134
Media Lab at MIT, 114, 117
merger, 35, 48–50
"Me So Horny" (2 Live Crew), 70
Microsoft, Inc., 48, 58, 65
Microsoft Windows, 48, 58
Miller, Carolyn, 105
Moore, Clayton, ix
Moore, Demi, 70
MOOs, 13, 127
moral rights, 123, 135
MUDs, 127
multimedia, 73, 115, 137
Murray, Charles, 5
Myers, Greg, 105
"My Seven Bizzos" (2 Live Crew), 70

Naked Gun 33 1/3, 70
national character, 4
national culture, 2, 3, 4, 81, 97, 131
National Information Infrastructure's (NII) White Paper. *See* NII White Paper
Nature of Copyright, The (Patterson and Lindberg), 143
nature of the work, the, 60, 73
Negroponte, Nicholas, 114, 117, 136, 142
NET Act. *See* No Electronic Theft Act
Net Culture, 94, 95
Netlaw: Your Rights in the Online World (Rose), 14
news reporting, 59, 61, 72–73
Nielsen, Leslie, 70
NII White Paper, 12, 18, 148, 153
1997 Copyright Extension Act, 45
1909 Copyright Revision Act, 36, 37

1976 Copyright Act, 12, 30, 35, 37, 40, 45, 55, 62, 78, 122, 124, 136, 141, 144, 145, 146
1976 House Report, 65, 66, 73, 74
No Electronic Theft Act (1988), 13, 79

"Oh, Pretty Woman" (Orbison), 6, 70
Orbison, Roy, 6, 70
originality, 31, 33, 35, 40, 50, 55–57
out-of-print works, 75
ownership, ix, xii, 8, 9, 22, 112, 113, 114, 115, 117, 118, 120, 122, 123, 125, 126, 127, 129, 135, 136, 145, 146, 147, 148

Pac-Man, 62
parody, 7, 59, 61, 67–72, 133
participatory democracy, 1, 88, 100, 110, 131, 142, 146, 147, 150
participatory government, 100, 102, 104, 147
patent, 33–39
Patent Act, 33
Patterson, L. Ray, 124, 143
plagiarism, 35, 50–52, 54
policy, 3, 4, 5, 6, 7, 8, 10, 15, 16, 18, 19, 20, 59, 77–83, 125, 131, 132, 143, 144, 145, 147, 148
policy purpose of constitutional provision, 36, 77–83, 132, 147, 148
positivism, 40, 107, 112
positivist interpretation, 99
Post, David, 15
primary constitutional goal, 37, 132, 139–40, 143, 144, 147
primary statutory goal, 140, 144
Princeton University Press v. Michigan Document Services, 67
proprietorship of knowledge, 112
protectionist stance, 2, 3, 40, 79, 92, 120, 125, 134, 137, 139, 153
protection of intellectual products, 27, 30, 33, 37, 40
public access, 2, 3, 5, 7, 8, 40, 59–76, 78, 79, 81, 88, 121, 123, 124, 125, 126, 127, 131, 132, 140, 147, 150

Publications Int'l Ltd. v. Bally Mfg. Corp., 62
public domain, 19, 37, 41, 56, 57, 60, 124, 136, 144
purpose and character of use, 59, 60, 61–62

quotation, 59, 62–64

rationalization, 106
reputation, 28–30
reverse engineering, 34, 35, 48–50
Rheingold, Howard, 108, 142, 143
right of access, 80
Romantic view, 10, 23, 113, 121, 126, 127, 131, 132, 135, 146, 147, 148
Romeo and Juliet, 47
Rose, Lance, 14
Rosenfeld, Harry N., 71
Rude, Carolyn, 18
Rushkoff, Douglas, 108, 142

Salinger, J. D., 63, 109
Samuelson, Pamela, 136, 137
scenes a faire, 58
Scientology, 63
scope of employment, 44, 46
Seinfeld, 70
Seinfeld Aptitude Test, The, 70
Shetland Times v. Wills, 65
Simpson, Bart, 133
Simpson, O. J., 71
Smith Act, 6
social constructionism, 87–111, 127, 132, 135, 147, 150
Social Psychology of Romantic Love, The, 72
Sonny Bono Copyright Extension Act (1999), 13
Sony Corp. v. Universal Studios, Inc., 75–76
Soviet Union, 141
standardized test sheets, 74–75
Strong, William, 63
substantial similarity, 35, 50–52, 57

Swan, Jim, 54
"sweat of the brow," 122, 135, 147

tangibility, 35, 40, 55, 77, 78, 136, 147
Ticketmaster v. Microsoft, 65
Timberg, Bernard, 105
trademark, 28–30, 88
trade secret, 30–33
Tristan und Isolde, 47
2 Live Crew, 67, 70

unpublished works, 75

Vanity Fair, 70
video production, 73–74

West, Susan, 18
West Side Story, 47
White-Smith Music Pub. Co. v. Apollo Co., 37
Windows. *See* Microsoft Windows
Woodmansee, Martha, 18
workbooks, 74–75
work for hire, 11, 17, 37–38, 41, 43–47
World Wide Web, 10, 12, 13, 17, 20, 21, 29, 30, 39, 40, 64, 65, 67, 130, 138, 139, 142, 145, 146, 152, 153
Writing Space (Bolter), 118

Zuboff, Shoshana, 115

TyAnna K. Herrington is an assistant professor in the School of Literature, Communication, and Culture at the Georgia Institute of Technology. Her background in law (J.D. 1985) contributes to her interest in intellectual property issues, although her specialization in rhetoric and technical communication (Ph.D. 1997) drives her ideological inquiry. Herrington has been teaching virtual classes since 1993 and was supported by a Fulbright grant to teach and collaboratively develop a distance learning project in St. Petersburg, Russia, in 1999. The Global Classroom Project in cross-curricular technical communication, currently under way, electronically links students in St. Petersburg, Russia, with those at Georgia Tech in Atlanta.